Asgrim pulled his sw... to the eerie attack. ... clearly: not as tall as ... gleam of predatory intelligence in its liquid black eyes. Asgrim's sword swept down – a leathery crack, a spurt of dark blood. The black eyes glazed.

The remaining five lizards spread out to encircle them. 'By Sinh, they have the cunning of wolves!' cursed Flügel, drawing his shortsword.

Even as he spoke, two of the lizards lunged forward from opposite sides while a third threw its spear . . .

Join Asgrim the barbarian as he sets off on a treacherous journey across the arid Wastes of Lagarto in search of the tomb of a dead tyrant – a tomb rumoured to be filled with treasure. Read carefully, for you too must prepare yourself for a heroic venture – a venture that will test your endurance and skills to the utmost . . .

HeroQuest: The Tyrant's Tomb is based on the bestselling fantasy board game, *HeroQuest*.

Also available by Dave Morris,
and published by Corgi Books:

HEROQUEST: THE FELLOWSHIP OF FOUR
HEROQUEST: THE SCREAMING SPECTRE

HEROQUEST

THE TYRANT'S TOMB

DAVE MORRIS

CORGI BOOKS

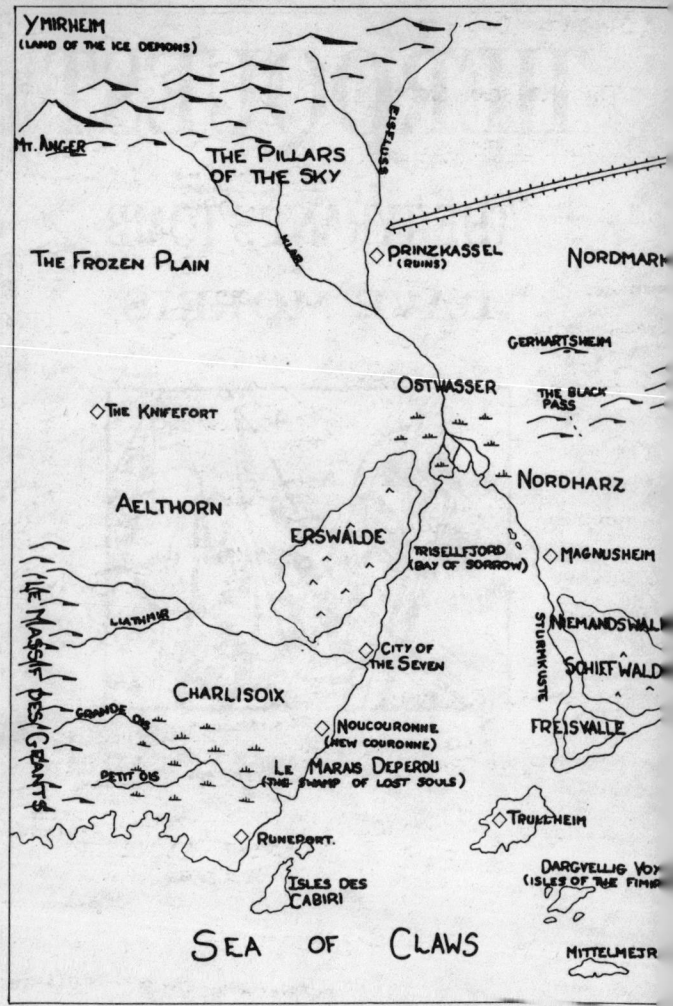

The HeroQuest World is loosely based on the Warhammer World which is the copyright of Games Workshop and is used with their permission.

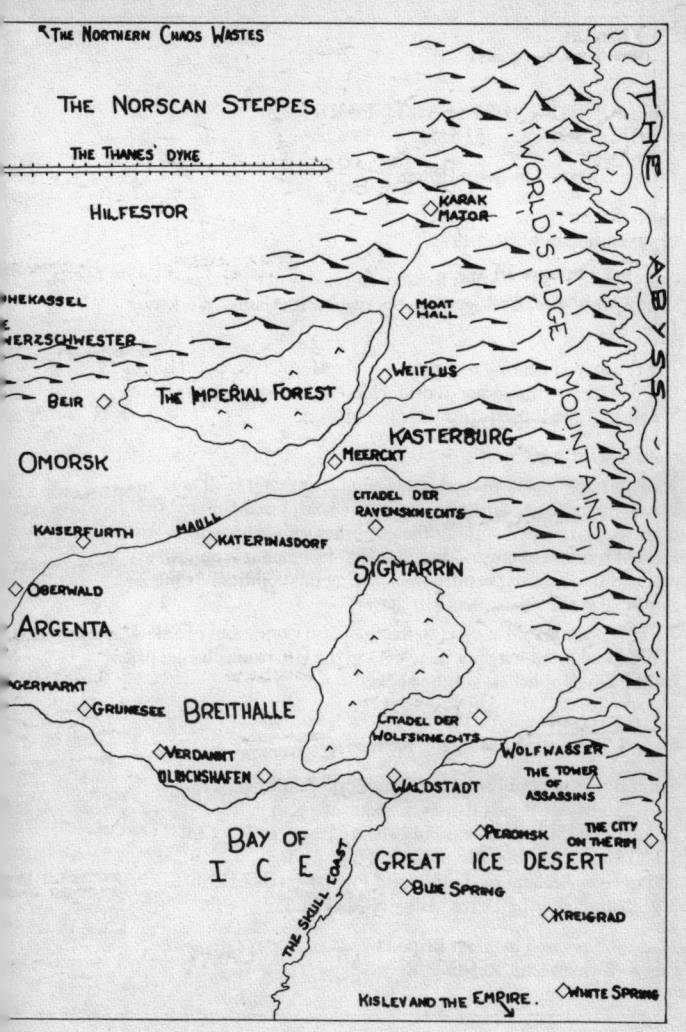

THE NORTHERN CHAOS WASTES

THE NORSCAN STEPPES

THE THANES' DYKE

HILFESTOR

KARAK MAJOR

MOAT HALL

HEKASSEL
NERZSCHWESTER

BEIR

THE IMPERIAL FOREST

WEIFLUS

KASTERBURG

OMORSK

MEERCKT

CITADEL DER
RAVENSKNECHTS

KAISERFURTH

MAULI

KATERINASDORF

OBERWALD

SIGMARRIN

ARGENTA

GERMARKT

GRUNESEE

BREITHALLE

CITADEL DER
WOLFSKNECHTS

VERDANINT
OLBICHSHAFEN

WALDSTADT

WOLFWASSER

THE TOWER
OF
ASSASSINS

BAY OF
I C E

THE SKULL COAST

GREAT ICE DESERT

PEROMSK

THE CITY
ON THE RIM

BLUE SPRING

KREIGRAD

KISLEV AND THE EMPIRE.

WHITE SPRING

WORLD'S EDGE MOUNTAINS

THE ABYSS

HEROQUEST: THE TYRANTS TOMB
A CORGI BOOK : 0 552 52777 7

First publication in Great Britain

PRINTING HISTORY
Corgi edition published 1993

Set in 11/12pt Linotype Plantin by
County Typesetters, Margate, Kent

Corgi Books are published by Transworld Publishers Ltd,
61–63 Uxbridge Road, Ealing, London W5 5SA,
in Australia by Transworld Publishers (Australia) Pty Ltd,
15–25 Helles Avenue, Moorebank, NSW 2170,
and in New Zealand by Transworld Publishers (NZ) Ltd,
3 William Pickering Drive, Albany, Auckland.

Made and printed in Great Britain by
Cox & Wyman Ltd, Reading, Berks.

THE TYRANT'S TOMB

CHAPTER ONE

The rocks were a jagged mass of blackness, resting on flat sands that the moonlight had turned into an immense white sea. A tall broad-shouldered figure rose to his feet and, drawing his thick fur cloak tighter about him, gazed down in brooding silence from his vantage point.

A hand tugged at his cloak. 'By Sinh, God of Thieves, get down, barbarian! They will see you.'

Asgrim stayed where he was, his eyes drinking in the details of the scene spread out beneath him in the moonlight. The hour might come when those silent sands would become his battleground, and he desired to know every detail of them.

A stone tomb stood a few hundred paces from the rocks where he and his companion hid – perhaps a bowshot's distance, if that bow were drawn by a strong man like Asgrim. Beyond it lay a few shattered columns and toppled domes, the last remnants of a mighty city that had stood here in times long gone. The tomb was low-roofed, shaped like a flat-topped pyramid, its ancient carvings scoured smooth by centuries of wind-blasted desert sand.

In front of the tomb were clustered the creatures who were the reason for Asgrim's sharp interest – and for his companion's fear. These were large two-legged lizards with keenly intelligent eyes. In their spindly forelimbs they carried simple spears, and they had harried Asgrim and Flügel with the cunning of wolf packs as they crossed the great Wastes of Lagarto. Now, though, the lizards had all assembled into a host of two hundred or more and were huddled together around a massive dark shape stretched out in front of the tomb.

The moon rose higher. A chill wind soughed over the barren plain, sifting the fine white dust and producing an eerie howl among the ruins beyond the tomb. Asgrim grunted sourly and hunkered down among the rocks.

Flügel gave a sigh of relief. 'They might have seen you,' he said, irritated at the barbarian's aloof disregard of his advice.

'They didn't.' Asgrim pulled the cloak around him and lay back against a rock, eyes heavy-lidded. To a casual glance it might have seemed that he was completely relaxed, even dozing. But any other fighting man would have recognized the latent energy coiled inside the barbarian's muscular frame. At the slightest sign of danger, he would be on his feet, brandishing his sword and ready for action.

'What now, then?' said Flügel challengingly. If the barbarian had a plan, he wanted to be in on it.

'We wait,' grunted Asgrim without opening his eyes.

There was a long pause. 'For what?' demanded Flügel, frustrated by his companion's laconic manner.

'Till dawn,' said Asgrim. 'Now the lizards are all huddled around something – a great log or somesuch. I couldn't make it out from here.'

'They're trying to conserve their body warmth,' said Flügel. At night the temperature could drop below freezing.

'Perhaps. Whatever, there's no point trying to take on a hundred of the devils. We'll wait till sunrise, when they disperse into packs to go foraging.'

Flügel envied the young barbarian his lithe and powerful physique. He himself was a misshapen lump: hunchbacked, and lame by reason of a club foot. Wherever he roamed, children ran behind him pelting him with taunts and sticks, while adults turned aside to hide their expressions of disgust. Small wonder, then, that Flügel had turned to a life of thievery. Since others were determined to make him the untrusted outcast, he reasoned, why not play that part to the hilt? And, despite his shuffling lopsided gait, Flügel was a skilled exponent of his chosen craft. His arms were strong, allowing him to climb well, and what he lacked in agility he compensated for with his small size and furtive cunning. How many fine merchants had turned up their noses at the sight of a shabby hunchback suddenly staggering as though drunk from an alleyway, never to notice the sharp knife that severed their purse-strings as they turned to hurry away?

Flügel gazed at Asgrim in the cold moonlight. The barbarian looked like a sculpted statue of marble. All

Flügel's self-congratulation evaporated in an instant. He would have set aside his larcenous profession without a qualm, even if it meant a life of poverty and hunger, to have a body that was well-formed and comely. But these were foolish fancies – the sort of daydreams Flügel had not indulged in since his childhood. Over the rocks lay their goal: the tomb of the tyrant Chungor Khan. Wealth awaited them within. Wealth to sate the avarice of the king of thieves! Soon, Flügel mused, he would be richer than any silk-clad merchant. Then let them turn their noses up at him. Let them try.

He shifted, placing his hand where he could feel the reassuring hilt of the shortsword under his cloak. They had a long wait ahead of them. Flügel was no stranger to waiting. He had often sat motionless for hours, cramped into uncomfortable positions, hiding in darkness for a light to go out or a shutter to be opened. Patience was more than a virtue among thieves; it was a professional skill.

Flügel looked up at the moon. A gleaming white pearl in a vault of black crystal. The cold dry air made the stars seem dazzlingly bright. He cast his mind back three months, to a night when the moon had been just as full, but hidden then behind a haze of cloud and chimney smoke. The night when he and Asgrim had first met . . .

It was in the fetid backstreets of Runeport, among the taverns with their narrow bottle-glass windows, the cobblestones outside slick with refuse and midden. Runeport had originally been established as a military garrison, a bleak coastal outpost south of the Swamp of Lost Souls, and soldiers with pay to spend and nowhere to go had little choice but to head to those grimy back alleys.

Flügel heard a cry of *'Gardez l'eau!'* and barely jumped back in time as a torrent of dirty water sloshed from an upstairs window and splattered the cobblestones where he had been standing. Flowing into the clogged gutter, it washed over his boots. He grimaced and scuffed them fastidiously against the wall. He watched potato peelings swirl like stranded boats in the muddy puddle. Only kitchen scraps, then. Flügel had had worse poured over him.

Hunger gnawed at him, but he fought the urge to grab some of the potato peelings. He had travelled far of late, with few opportunities to ply his craft, and his purse sagged sadly empty. Tonight he would have to earn a few coins. The soldiers were poor pickings: too often they got much of their pay in the form of credit notes, not hard cash. All the same, they would supply enough for Flügel's current needs. In a few months, if all went well, he would never again know the sting of hunger or poverty.

Flügel approached a tavern. The usual stink and clamour spilled out through the half-open door. He pushed it open and went inside, eyes immediately smarting from the acrid pipeweed smoke. Flügel cursed the Brettonians and the outlandish ways that had been imported from some of their other colonies. There had been a time, he recalled, when at least one could get a drink of ale without choking in this rancid fog.

He lurched towards the bar, a half-unnoticed figure among the tall laughing soldiers and their ladies. The few that glanced his way were quick to avert their eyes from the unwelcome ugly wretch in their midst.

It seemed his lameness made him stumble against someone: a soldier still in his tabard from the parade ground, with curling blond moustache waxed back against his cheeks. Long familiarity made Flügel tolerant of the mercurial Brettonian insults that were flung at his back. Words no longer had any power to hurt him. Besides, he now had the soldier's money pouch up his grubby sleeve.

'Watch where you're going, can't you?'

Flügel looked up sharply. The remark had not been directed at him, but at a tall youth in a jerkin of studded leather standing at the bar. From his long black hair and pale skin, Flügel judged him to be a native of these northlands. His jerkin and Brettonian longsword marked him as a mercenary.

The youth turned his head slowly, met the man's gaze. Unhurriedly he brushed spilt ale from his arm. 'You bumped into me,' he said.

The soldier who had jostled him turned to his friends with a grin. 'Hear that? The barbarian knows a few words of civilized speech.'

'Aye, but no civilized manners,' said one of the others. They all laughed. They looked like a pack of dogs with their too-bright eyes and too-loud bluster.

Despite his youth, the barbarian had more sense than to be baited by them. 'No,' he said, 'I would not say I have the manners of you civilized men.' He turned away, raising the tankard to his lips.

The soldier caught his arm. 'What do you mean by that?' he growled, brave enough when he knew his friends were with him. 'Do you mean to insult us, you northern lout?'

The barbarian looked at the hand. The soldier's fingers barely half encircled the thick muscle of his

14

forearm. He turned his gaze up. Cold grey eyes, filled with the force of Norse winters and hard steel, gleamed in the smoky lantern-light. 'You insult your own honour every time you open your mouth,' he said coolly. 'Now remove your hand, or I'll add injury to that insult.'

One of the other men laughed at this 'Oh ho, Guillarme, this barbarian lad has a keen enough wit, I'll give him that!'

The soldier called Guillarme bared his teeth. 'You scum—' he hissed at the barbarian. But he removed his hand from the other's arm.

'Come on, Guillarme,' said another of them, tugging at his sleeve. 'Leave the lad alone. It's your turn to get the drinks in!'

'Trust Guillarme to pick a squabble when it's his round!' chortled a third soldier.

The barbarian turned away, bored by this 'civilized' prattle. No doubt, reflected Flügel, men of his homeland had better things to talk about over their drinks. Great tales of glory, or the recounting of death duels, perhaps.

Enraged that his friends' jocularity was now being enjoyed at his own expense, Guillarme acted more rashly than he might have if he had paused for sober thought. He took a step back, hand on the pommel of his sword. 'You spill my drink, then insult me,' he railed at the young barbarian. 'Now you think to ignore me! By the gods, Norscan, is that sword you wear at your side only for show?'

At last the barbarian turned and gave Guillarme his full attention. He drew up straight, looming as big as a bear. Flügel saw Guillarme visibly quail behind his mask of bravado.

The others set down their goblets, also touching the pommels of their weapons. The barbarian looked from one to the other. He counted four men ready to fight. He said: 'Among my people, the sword is held in high esteem. It is not thought glorious to draw it over the spilling of a puddle of ale.'

Guillarme took in the words, gradually losing his expression of sickly nervousness. He supposed the barbarian was backing down from the fight, and sheer relief made him push his luck too far. 'So,' he said, throwing back his head with a sneer, 'here is a barbarian who will not sully his sword in a tavern brawl. How squeamish of him – and how convenient, eh?'

The barbarian shrugged. 'I have no such qualms about using my hands, however.'

Guillarme had no time to react. The barbarian's left fist came up and caught him hard in the pit of the stomach. He curled up around the blow with a sound like he was about to vomit. The barbarian drew back his arm, paused long enough to take a draught from the tankard still held in his other hand, then delivered a second punch, this time to the chin, of such force that it lay Guillarme out flat across the bar like a cod on a fishmonger's stall.

Silence fell like a blanket. For a moment nobody moved. Flügel watched the frozen tableau: a lone barbarian, strong-thewed with the look of a wild wolf, facing three soldiers with too much beer in their bellies. It would be no even fight, if Flügel was any judge of such brawls. Those Norscans were all but born with a sword in their hands, whereas the soldiers of the garrison were flabby townsmen who thought that six months' basic training and a scruffy

16

uniform were enough to make a man a warrior. But the tavern was packed with dozens of soldiers – mostly troops recruited locally – and they were the sort to draw courage from numbers. No matter how fiercely the barbarian fought, eventually he would be overwhelmed.

Flügel edged over to the door. The instant of tension exploded into activity as blades scraped from scabbards. The barbarian opened his mouth to give the battle roar of his people.

Flügel cupped his hands to his mouth and bellowed with all the strength in his lungs: 'Night Watch! Lay down your weapons!'

The effect on the patrons of the tavern was remarkable. Forgetting the barbarian, they spilled out of every available exit like frightened rats and went scurrying off into the darkness. Flügel had to dodge aside as one fellow – a trader in a velvet jerkin – jumped up to dive through the narrow window. 'Out of my way, cripple!' the man cried. 'I've no wish to languish in the Watch's jail, even if you have!'

In less than a minute, the tavern had emptied. The barbarian stood alone amid the debris of spilled tankards and overturned stools. The soldiers had disappeared out of the back door behind the bar, dragging their unconscious friend Guillarme with them.

Flügel dragged his lame leg over to the bar. 'I'd put that sword away if I were you, barbarian,' he said with a grotesque grin. 'The Night Watch might get the wrong idea.'

The barbarian glanced at the empty doorway, then sheathed his sword. 'That was you?' he said.

Flügel righted a stool and clambered up on to it. 'Half of these lowlifes are wanted for some petty villainy or other. The rest cannot risk arrest: the penalty for using your sword in an affray is branding.'

The barbarian nodded thoughtfully. 'So you have saved me from a branding . . .' He turned back to his tankard of ale.

Flügel laughed wryly. 'Not in your case. A Brettonian could expect to be branded. A barbarian like yourself they would simply hang.'

'Among my people, whom you call "barbarian", justice is dispensed equally to strangers as to friends. Apparently the law of civilization is not like that.'

'It is closer to divine law,' said Flügel with some bitterness. The youth looked at him, and he went on: 'The same justice that gives a straight back and a pleasing face to a man like that Guillarme, but fashions another man lame and ugly as Flügel Mooncalf.'

'Fate, neither cruel nor kind, takes no notice of our lives. I myself was once respected among my people, the Valrings. But Fate conspired to make me a kin-slayer and an outcast.'

Flügel poured himself a goblet from the flagon on the bar. 'Let us drink to Fate, then, barbarian, which tonight has been kind to us both. For I have travelled long and far to find a comrade with a strong sword-arm and a dauntless heart.'

The barbarian looked at him with a new keenness. 'It sounds as if you have some undertaking in mind.'

Flügel nodded, smiling, and raised his cup. 'An undertaking that could make us rich beyond our dreams. You'll be as bent-backed as I, barbarian, under the weight of treasure you'll take away from this venture!'

The barbarian pondered a moment, then touched his tankard to Flügel's cup with a leaden chink. 'My name is Asgrim,' he said.

CHAPTER TWO

Red sunlight sizzled down, making the rocks a kiln. Asgrim cast off his furs and stretched.

Flügel watched him with narrowed eyes, his drab clothing already sticky with sweat. 'It's dawn,' he said. 'Do we go in now?'

Asgrim hoisted himself up on to the shelf of rock, his shoulder muscles rippling as he hung there studying the plain in front of the tomb. 'The lizards are stirring,' he said. 'The sun's heat gives them the vitality they need to go foraging. Soon . . .' He dropped back from the rock.

Flügel had gone off a little distance to perform his morning toilet. Suddenly he gave a muffled yelp of astonishment and came scurrying back. He had what looked like a scrap of greenish-brown leather in his hand. It crackled drily as he held it up to show Asgrim.

'What is it?' said the barbarian.

'The discarded skin of one of those lizards, I

think,' said Flügel. He drew it over his head and shoulders like a cloak, and now Asgrim could clearly see the distinctive tail and legs of a bipedal lizard. 'They must shed their skins like snakes.'

Asgrim shrugged disinterestedly. He tore a piece of jerky from the provisions in his satchel and chewed it as he buckled on his sword and dagger. Despite the growing heat of the day, he donned his jacket of studded leather and his steel vambraces. 'Within the tomb it will be cool enough,' he explained to Flügel.

'You expect to need armour once we're inside?' asked Flügel uncertainly.

Asgrim gave a grim smile. 'I have heard enough tales from men who tried to plunder the riches of the dead. Those ancient tombs are often protected – usually by the most grisly of guardians.'

As he secured the straps of the armour, Asgrim found himself thinking of how he had been drawn into this ambitious venture. A chance acquaintance with a crippled thief, a narrow scrape with Brettonian soldiers, a few cups of wine and tales of gold . . .

Asgrim thought ruefully of the life he might have led. A life of battle-glory and the proper plunder of war. His arms might have gleamed with gold given him honourably, by his father or other war-chiefs, to reward him for valour and fine deeds. Instead he was an exile, a lordless vagabond, forced to hire his sword to those who would buy it. Those were men for whom honour was a thing to be bought and sold. Their victories were won with intrigue and bribery more often than with naked steel. Asgrim trusted them as much as he did carrion-crows, and each day

he spent in a city left a taste of vileness in his mouth
that no cheap tavern water could wash away.

So it was that he had been fair game for the
vaunting schemes of Flügel the thief . . .

'Do you understand me, barbarian?' Flügel had said.
'The gold and gems of that lost place will make us
richer than kings!'

Intrigued despite himself, Asgrim had brushed
back his long mane of black hair and pondered
Flügel's words. They were sitting in the room
Asgrim had rented: a tiny garret over a dyer's shop.
The dyes had a sharp reek, but Asgrim preferred it
to the smells of the city streets. 'I'll hear more,' he
said. 'Who was he, this dead king of whom you
speak?'

'Chungor Khan,' Flügel repeated. 'By many
accounts, the most direful despot ever to inflict his
rule on the lands of men. His empire stretched
further than any before or since, and his soldiers
enforced his will upon his people as though it were
the will of the gods. As his power grew, so did his
cruelty, and stories of his tyranny are well known.
When one of Chungor Khan's tax collectors kept
back a few coins for himself, the tyrant, learning of
this, had the wretch dragged before his throne. The
Khan said he was a generous man and he'd give the
tax collector all the gold he could eat. The man was
forced to swallow gold coins, then the tyrant's
soldiers threw him into a pool. Chungor Khan only
laughed, swimming with his concubines as the tax
collector drowned at the bottom of his pool.'

'It sounds like tap-room prattle to me,' muttered
Asgrim. 'Where would one madman get such power?

22

His own courtiers would poison him rather than suffer such indignities!'

'He made a pact with the snake goddess Meretseger,' Flügel told him. 'She agreed to give him three gifts, and in return he would pile her altars full of human sacrifices. Many screamed as they were flayed alive in homage to the snake goddess. Many skulls were hurled into her sacred pit.'

'Yes,' said Asgrim impatiently. 'And the gifts the Khan received?'

'Power to reign as absolute tyrant, such that no living man could ever overcome him. Wealth to fill his treasuries, greater than all the lost hoards that lie on the ocean depths. And a third gift . . . It must have been a secret between the Khan and his goddess; I can find no mention of it in the ancient legends.'

The young barbarian smiled a sceptical smile. 'There are other such tales. If I had a silver piece for each I've heard, I'd be a richer man than I am now.'

Flügel shook his head insistently. 'The people of the hinterland still huddle around their firesides in fear of the tyrant, even to this day. His very name instils such dread that a peasant of the western lands will make the sign of the protective eye at the mention of him. And they will never discuss any sickness or misfortune when a snake is nearby, for fear it will bear such tidings to Chungor Khan and his goddess and bring disaster on their heads.'

'That sounds a sensible enough precaution,' allowed Asgrim, who like any barbarian had a healthy respect for superstition. 'It is always wise to avoid the attention of the gods. But it gives no proof that this Chungor Khan ever existed. Indeed, if your story is true and the snake goddess made him unconquerable by mortal man, I wonder how it was he met his doom?'

'It should have been old age,' said Flügel, 'but it was not. Mere whim took the tyrant on a journey to the very westernmost edge of his realm. This was deep into the arid plains that men now call the Wastes of Lagarto. They rode for a score of days, boiled by the sun and frozen by the icy nights, and many of his entourage fell by the wayside. But Chungor Khan only laughed at their distress and called them weaklings, driving his courtiers further and further into the west. At last, having passed the last oasis and the last nomad tribe who rendered him tribute, the Khan demanded to know what lay beyond. His courtiers did not know what to say, for who had ever ventured so far west? But his vizier, fearing to show ignorance to his lord, declared that only the evening sun dwelt there. "The evening sun!" cried the Khan with a fierce laugh. "He has gold aplenty; I've seen it on his shield. We'll ride on and demand tribute from him."'

'Now that,' said Asgrim, 'was an unlucky thing to say.'

Flügel nodded. 'Indeed. For towards dusk they saw a man in golden armour riding on a palamino, its gilt-trimmed barding glittering in the sunset. This knight's lance was couched for battle, but the Khan waved back his warriors. He would face the man alone. Taking up his spear and sword, fearless because of his deodate invulnerability, he urged his mount into a charge. They rushed together, the spears clashed, and each found its mark in the other's heart. The Khan sank from his steed with a groan,

24

amazed to see his lifeblood ebbing away into the dry dust. His opponent fell silently, and when his visor was lifted the courtiers discovered a cadaver within, skin cured like jerky by the arid desert winds.'

'So the tyrant was slain, but not by any living man,' said Asgrim approvingly. 'That is the way the gods work.'

'His attendants must have thought so. Feeling his death to be the result of supernatural design, they journeyed on into the west until they came to a ruined city. The vizier decreed this to be the palace of the evening sun, and there they built the tyrant's tomb. They placed his body within, and with it every item of gold and jewels that he possessed – for they feared the wrath of Chungor Khan even beyond the grave. Then they sealed the tomb and so it has remained throughout the centuries since.'

'Ah, but there's the nub of the matter,' said Asgrim. 'How do you know the story is true? And why shouldn't others have looted the place since?'

'I was in Tarkesh Varn, a fortress city in the far west beyond the Titan Hills. There I heard two nomads of the desert fringes discussing the legend, and one told of having seen the tomb. He said it was guarded by a dragon and a race of werelizards.'

Asgrim nodded. 'And your reason for supposing this tale to be true?'

'When the nomads realized I had overheard their conversation, they tried to kill me.' Flügel smiled. 'They revere the snake goddess and fear her retribution.'

Asgrim was finally convinced – as he had wanted to be all along, his headstrong lust for adventure being stronger than his doubts. And so they had set out, encountering a host of hazards on their journey west. The marshy moors outside Runeport hid a dozen dangers, including web-fingered goblins who sculled about in coracles of human skin. Asgrim and Flügel set an ambush and sent a horde of the loathsome creatures down to rot in the river mud. In the Titan Hills they had to contend with ogres hurling rocks down from the heights, and a troll which lurked under a great bridge of stone and demanded a fee before he would allow them to cross. Asgrim gave him his payment in cold steel.

Finally they had arrived at the citadel of Tarkesh Varn, the last farflung outpost of civilization before the desolate Wastes of Lagarto. The journey from Runeport had taken a month . . .

Soldiers had watched them with disinterest as they clambered the steep path to the fort and trudged in under the ancient lintel of the east gate. Asgrim studied the soldiers' grey and blue livery and wondered what allegiance it indicated.

'Tarkesh Varn is claimed by no-one,' said Flügel. 'The citizens raise a small militia from among their own people, but they are not part of any nation.'

One of the soldiers stepped forward and said in a bored voice, 'There is a toll to enter the citadel.'

After some haggling, the toll was paid and they passed on into the citadel. Tarkesh Varn was a place of thick grey walls and crooked gravel-strewn streets. Pale gold sunlight slanted past its towers and hung over the streets in a sere haze. Fine dust from the desert found its way on to every surface and soon sifted into their clothing.

Asgrim and Flügel walked on in silence, dazzled by even this forlorn oasis of habitation after their long solitary journey. Under wooden awnings, stall-holders displayed their meagre wares on benches lining the street, but showed no inclination to tout for business from two impoverished wanderers. Children and chickens rummaged in the dry dirt. Women walked by with clay pitchers on their heads, bearing water from the spring at the bottom of the hill outside the east gate.

They found lodging in an inn beside a small courtyard paved with flagstones. The innkeeper was a sallow, pinch-featured man who took their coins and showed them to beds of hard baked clay beside the hearth. There he dumped their haversacks unceremoniously and pointed to a steaming kettle over the fire. 'You may help yourselves to cups of boiling water, within reason,' he announced. 'It can be flavoured with iris petals for an additional sum, or drunk as it is. Breakfast comprises a salted griddle-cake served with a garnish of garlic juice. Its apparent meagreness may alarm you, but it is remarkably sustaining. Other meals are extra.'

'We have some provisions of our own,' said Flügel, anxious to conserve their savings so as to purchase a couple of mounts.

The innkeeper viewed him askance. 'That is irregular,' he said. 'Naturally we must levy a surcharge for the use of cooking facilities.'

After further negotiation, more coins were paid over and the innkeeper went back to the front of his establishment. Asgrim and Flügel were left to inspect the remainder of their finances.

'Five guilders!' snorted Asgrim. 'It will not buy us one horse, let alone two.'

Flügel considered the options. 'We could buy

some pack mules,' he suggested. 'That should leave us with enough to buy tents and provisions. We'll also need some tools for excavating the tomb: shovels, pick-axes, and so on.'

They went out, ostensibly to shop, but a morbid interest drew them to the west gate. Both were keen to gaze upon the desert they must cross to reach their goal. Passing the stalls and the mule market, they reached the heavy shadow of the city wall. The west gate was a long low-ceilinged tunnel leading through to the inhospitable Wastes of Lagarto. Asgrim had to stoop to walk along it, hearing his footsteps echo in the gloom. Dusty sunlight filtered down enough to show deep score-marks in the stone of the tunnel walls: the bored etching of city guards, the despairing sentiments of those sent into exile through this gate in ages past.

They emerged into fierce sunlight and a roaring arid wind. A monolith of red granite stood directly outside the gateway, so that they had to walk around it to get a view of the desert.

'See the carvings on its surface,' said Flügel, pointing at the monolith. 'Like runes. What is it for, I wonder?'

'To shield the tunnel from this scouring wind,' said Asgrim. He reached the edge of the monolith and had to bow his head, hand raised to shield his eyes from dust. Flügel trudged up behind him, forcing his way against the wind. Together they surveyed the scene.

The Wastes of Lagarto were a featureless plain of grit. The rocks and dust showed no colour, only varying shades of grey. The gale whipping off this barren land seemed eager to steal all moisture, driving hard dry fingers into every crack in their clothing and running its rough hide over their skin.

'The wind is worst at dawn and dusk,' called Flügel over the shrieking gale. 'We'll travel by night, when the temperature drops to freezing. Exertion will keep us warm, but you'll need your Norscan furs as well. By day, the sun heats the plain like a kiln; it's then we'll pitch our tents and sleep.'

Asgrim nodded, spitting dust, and pulled his companion back into the lee of the monolith. 'You've planned this trip thoroughly,' he said.

'Would you rather I'd come to you with vague notions and unformed schemes?' countered Flügel. 'No, barbarian – I need you as my partner to deal with those threats and obstacles that call for courage and a strong body. But do not suppose that Flügel Mooncalf cannot pull his weight. My careful planning will stand us in good stead.'

They wasted no time on the scant comforts of the inn, but hastened with their preparations so that on the next evening they were ready to set out. Their money had bought four mules, which Asgrim led firmly by their reins while Flügel followed on behind to give encouragement, when it was needed, in the form of a sharp birch.

Under fading sunlight, the desert resembled a drawing in ochre. Wind screeched out of the west bearing stinging handfuls of grit. They bent into the distant red haze marking the horizon and began their crossing.

As the daylight went, the wind gradually dropped, leaving the sky clear and black as polished jet. One by one the stars appeared: steadily shining baubles. Flügel pointed at one. 'The Pole Star,' he said.

'There, in the constellation of the Gryphon. Keep it to your right.'

Time trickled on. They exchanged few words, listening to their own hushed footfalls and the crunch of the mules' hoofs in the dust. Other than that, the region was lifeless and silent. Blackness hung like a curtain all around them, just a pace or two beyond the lantern-light; they might have been actors miming motion on a darkened stage. Hours passed, and then a cold white glow behind them presaged the moonrise. A crescent of silver slid into the sky. Its light expanded the isolated circle illuminated by their lanterns, revealing a landscape of gravel-dunes and weirdly wind-etched boulders.

The wind rose towards dawn, thundering clouds of grey sand against their backs. Using a mound of rocks for shelter, they pitched a low tent and crawled under it. The temperature climbed, making their sleep sporadic and restless. When the sun set again, Flügel prepared a kettle of boiling water and they ate their rations sparingly.

Asgrim spat into the fire. 'By Eerg the All-Father, how long will we have to endure this dreary hell?'

'We may be able to cover five leagues each night,' said Flügel. 'The moon will be full by the time we reach the tomb.'

'And then there's the journey back,' said Asgrim, nodding sourly. He preferred any wild foe or icy windswept heath to such a lifeless wasteland.

'That will be less tedious,' said Flügel with a smile, getting to his feet. 'Our packloads of gold will provide much merriment.'

And so the days passed, running together like the dust patterns on the dunes. They became night creatures, hushed and shambling, shunning the day which brought such bitter heat. The cold of the night was numbing, but bearable. Worse was the absence of any living thing. Not even insects descended from the sky to seek their sweat. They began to feel cut off from the true world, as though trudging through the borderland of dreams. And so it took Asgrim a moment or two to come to his senses when, uncounted days out from Tarkesh Varn, a spear clattered off the gravel by his feet.

Six slender green figures came bounding noiselessly out of the sunset. They were two-legged lizards, with scaly crests erect above their necks and red tongues flickering from silently hissing mouths. In their small grasping forelimbs they carried crude spears and knives of flint.

Asgrim pulled his sword from its scabbard, reacting at last to the eerie attack. As the first lizard leapt in, he saw it clearly: not as tall as a man, but with strong sinews and the gleam of predatory intelligence in its liquid black eyes. Asgrim's sword swept down – a leathery crack, a spurt of dark blood. The black eyes glazed.

The remaining five lizards spread out to encircle them. 'By Sinh, they have the cunning of wolves!' cursed Flügel, drawing his shortsword.

Even as he spoke, two of the lizards lunged forward from opposite sides while a third threw its spear. Flügel gave a whimper as the spear ripped his fur clothing. He ducked back, his foot sliding in the gravel, and almost fell. The mishap saved him from being clawed by one of the lizards, which had jumped up to use the powerful claws of its hind legs. It went flying past the sprawling hunchback and

31

collided with Asgrim, who seized it in one brawny arm and swung it high over his shoulder, using it to swat at the lizard attacking him as a gladiator might swing his net against a foe. The two lizards fell and lay stunned, writhing in the dust. Asgrim despatched them quickly and hauled Flügel to his feet.

Three of the creatures were left. Asgrim and Flügel stood ready to face them, but no attack came. Instead the lizards turned their eyes to the fading daylight and then, with a final croaking hiss of defiance, they went loping away across the sands with jerking whip-tailed bounds.

That was not the last that they were to see of the bizarre lizard-creatures. Attacks became increasingly common as they pressed further across the desert. Always the lizards hunted in small groups – never more than six – and they seemed to roam only by day. Flügel took to setting traps when they settled down to sleep each daybreak, but these proved hardly necessary. Usually they were given ample alert of a lizard attack by the braying of the mules.

'What can they live on, out here in the Wastes?' wondered Asgrim as he skewered the last of a particularly tenacious band. 'I've seen no living thing but them.'

Flügel wiped the black blood off his shortsword. 'Perhaps the different bands hunt one another. If they are intelligent enough to make tools, they may be organized into tribes.'

Asgrim walked over to one of the mules. It had taken a spear in the side during the mêlée and now sagged to its knees, uttering weak snorts as its blood ran out. He raised his sword and finished it off.

'That leaves us with only three mules!' protested

Flügel. 'They'll have to carry all the treasure we find, *and* our provisions for the march back!'

Asgrim knelt and started hacking at the carcass with his knife, laying out thin strips of meat for the sun and wind to cure. 'These rations may do us more good than an extra packload of booty,' he grunted. 'I've no wish to be the richest corpse between here and Tarkesh Varn!'

CHAPTER THREE

 Asgrim again lifted himself up to the shelf of rock from which he could survey the tomb. 'That dragon you said you'd heard mentioned,' he said. '*That's* what they were huddled around.'

This brought Flügel scrambling up beside him. Despite his twisted body, the thief was an agile climber. He stared down at the great black shape basking in the sun. It was at least thirty paces long and might have been carved of obsidian, except for the slow twitching of its tail.

'That's no dragon,' he whispered. 'It's akin to a cockodrille. Sailors bring them up from Araby, but smaller than that one and stuffed.'

'It looks like a dragon to me.'

Flügel glared at him. The barbarian's stubbornness had annoyed him more and more during the endless days and nights crossing the desert. 'Have you ever seen a dragon?' he demanded irritably.

'Have you?' replied Asgrim.

Most of the lizards had dispersed into the desert. Only a few remained. They scurried forward to the cockodrille and performed a strange ritual: the giant reptile would first raise its snout, sniffing at the lizard in front of it. Then, apparently satisfied, it opened its jaws and the lizard would toss in a small morsel of food before turning and bounding away for the day's foraging.

'Like a king receiving tribute,' said Flügel. He suddenly noticed Asgrim was no longer beside him, but had dropped back down and was descending from the rocks. The thief hurried to catch up, and together they emerged on to the pebble-strewn plain in front of the tomb.

The last lizard had gone. The cockodrille lay in front of the tomb entrance, slumbering in the sun. They would have to pass it somehow. Asgrim drew his sword.

Hearing the grate of steel, the reptile raised its head. Its long jaws gaped in a cold grin, revealing teeth like flint knives. Scraps of the tribute it was fed still clung to those teeth: bloody tatters of meat and crunched insects, giving its breath the rank odour of carrion.

Asgrim stepped nearer. The reptile heaved its bulk around on short strong legs. Its scaly hide shone like wrought iron in the sunlight.

'It's still torpid from the night's chill,' Flügel realized. 'Its blood takes longer to warm up than the lizards'. Strike now, barbarian – each second you delay, it gets stronger!'

Asgrim needed no urging. When danger threatened, no warrior of his people was reluctant to enter the fray. The slow death was what they feared: death

35

by disease, death by old age. To meet your doom in battle was an end devoutly to be desired. Then the Valkyries, dainty nymphs on phantom steeds, would take the slain warrior's shade off to their halls where he could enjoy an eternity of feasting and fighting. The man who died a peaceful death, on the other hand, could expect only stark oblivion.

Asgrim's battle-cry split the ponderous silence between the ruins. His sword sheared down through the air, a sun-grazed arc. As it met the cockodrille's flanks, there was a sound as though he had struck a huge old oak: a leathery thunk, and the blade was turned aside, barely biting those hard black scales.

The reptile's jaws closed like a man-trap, just missing Asgrim's leg as he dodged back out of reach. He circled round, forcing the creature to turn the whole weight of its huge body around in order to keep its gaze on him. It moved sluggishly, but with tremendous force. There was no doubt that a single bite from those massive jaws could sever a man's spine.

Seeing his chance, Asgrim again dived in and landed two heavy blows before he was forced to back off. Neither showed as more than a score-mark across the armouring of scales.

'Perhaps you were right, Flügel,' he muttered; 'no dragon of legend was as impervious as this beast.'

For his part, Flügel kept well clear of the battle. This was his reason for bringing the barbarian, so that *he* could take such risks. 'The heroes who fought dragons used a spear,' he yelled. 'Perhaps its hide is easier to impale than to cut.'

Asgrim did not spare the breath for a retort. It had already occurred to him that a thrust might prove more effective, but a manoeuvre like that with his sword would leave him off-balance and in poor position to retreat. So he would have to make any thrust count. He circled as he sized up the likely weak points. The underbelly was an obvious choice, but the reptile's stance was lumbering and low to the ground; he might feint and dodge all day without getting an opening. Driving his sword into the open jaws was a more hopeful choice, but the creature's night-cooled torpor apparently did not extend to the long fang-filled jaws, which snapped shut again and again as if powered by steel springs. Asgrim narrowed his gaze as he moved warily closer. He held his sword in a two-handed grip, poised to drive it into the back of the gaping mouth and – if Fate so chose – on into the reptile's brain before it had the chance to bite.

A rock sailed past the cockodrille and clattered on the hard sun-baked dirt. It turned and gave a fluting growl, peering in the direction of the sound.

Sudden understanding dawned. It was *blind*. Anciently old, it relied on its other senses. That was why it had sniffed at each of the lizards as they presented their tribute. That was why it turned to face the rock Flügel had just thrown.

Asgrim knew that he had to act soon. The heat of the day was giving speed and vitality to his foe – while he, in his armour, felt his own strength being steadily sapped. His boot crunched on the dry grit, pulling the reptile's attention back towards him. Its cloudy pebble-eyes rolled as it strained to see him.

The barbarian edged forward, but not to deliver a blow. As he got almost within reach of those terrible jaws, he cast his sword over the reptile's head. It landed with a clatter on the ground, and instantly the huge saurian head swung around to snap at where the sound had come from.

Asgrim lunged. The cockodrille realized its mistake and turned back, jaws closing blindly. Asgrim gave a short cry of pain as he felt fangs sink into the flesh of his thigh, but the pain did not stop him getting his arms around the giant reptile's neck. He locked his hands under its throat as it bucked and rolled, forcing the hard heels of his hands up into the soft skin beside its windpipe. With titanic strength, the reptile lifted him up clear of the ground, frantically jolting him to and fro and trying to dash him against the stone wall of the tomb. Still Asgrim clung on, taking each bruising impact with just a scornful snort. Nothing would shake him free now. Even if his foe crushed his bones to powder, he would cling there until he choked the life out of it.

Gradually, its strength spent in frenzied writhing, the cockodrille sagged to the ground. Its jaws opened and closed feebly. Its tail swished, raging against the inevitable end. Asgrim crushed its neck with all the might in his brawny arms, ignoring his injuries, locked in an embrace of death. The red haze of the berserker rage rose across his vision . . .

'Barbarian! Barbarian! It's dead.'

Asgrim glared at him, his teeth bared like a beast's, and the little hunchback flinched back. The barbarian's eyes held a light that was scarcely human: the gleeful death-gleam of a demon out of hell. Flügel feared for his life. But then the berserker rage cleared, and Asgrim recognized his companion. He released his grip on the inert body and rolled away with a sigh.

Flügel took no chances. He first drove his short-sword up to the hilt into the cockodrille's eye, and only then went to assist Asgrim.

The barbarian was covered with a dozen grazes where the reptile had swung him against rock or sand, but it was the wound in his thigh that was most serious. Flügel poured on a stinging concoction from his hipflask and then bound the leg with a strip of cloth.

'Can you walk?' he said.

'Since the alternative is to lie here and rot: yes,' said Asgrim. He got to his feet, his teeth gritted at the stabbing pain, and hobbled over to retrieve his sword.

Flügel examined the carcass. It looked like a huge fallen tree, dry black bark splattered with blood-soaked dust. He tugged out his sword and as he did the jaws lolled open. They were almost big enough to swallow the little thief whole. 'Sinh, perhaps it *was* a dragon!' he said.

'No, you were right,' said Asgrim wearily. 'Couldn't choke a dragon to death.'

They went over to the tomb. There was a partially fallen colonnade, the remains of a mortuary temple built on to the side of the tomb. Flügel went and fetched the mules from their hiding place among the rocks and led them in under the colonnade out of the sun. Meanwhile, Asgrim had found a short tunnel clogged with sand which appeared to lead into the interior of the tomb. He unstrapped a spade from one of the mules and set to work, quickly clearing enough of the tunnel for them to enter.

The tunnel led to an oblong chamber smelling of rock dust. Little sunlight filtered in this far. Flügel kindled a lantern and lifted it, sending a flickering yellow beam swaying around the walls. Bright murals displayed scenes from the tyrant's life. There were images of blood-drenched conquest, with Chungor Khan in his chariot at the head of a vast army. Great cities were sieged and razed at his decree. Vanquished lords were shown bowing humbly at the Khan's feet. Other murals depicted the same lords being disembowelled on the altar of the snake goddess.

'The dry air has preserved them,' said Flügel, running his hand across the murals.

Asgrim had given them only a cursory glance, and now stooped to inspect the heavy clay jars arranged around the sides of the room.

'They could contain fine wines or oils,' suggested Flügel. 'Or gold dust . . .' His eyes goggled greedily in the lamplight.

Asgrim struck out with the spade, smashing open one of the jars. Fine yellow grains sifted out. 'Not gold, just sand,' grunted the barbarian. He got up and went to look for a route on, further into the tomb. 'Bring the light over here,' he called back to Flügel.

Flügel had been keen to examine the jars of sand, perhaps curious as to their purpose, but he came shuffling over and played the lantern over the rear wall of the chamber. A stone slab seemed to demark the outlines of a doorway. The slab had been chiselled into a bas-relief of Chungor Khan seated on his throne, staring imperiously out at them from the stone with a sneer of cold command.

'The sculptor read that madman's passions well,' commented Asgrim. 'Greed and cruelty and the blind desire for conquest. They form a mixture as dangerous as Chaos itself. I shall enjoy the task of hacking his lordly visage away.'

Asgrim went back to the mules and returned carrying a pack of tools. He had the pickaxe already in his hand. Flügel, meanwhile, had found two metal dishes hanging from chains in the ceiling, one on either side of the door. They looked like the weighing-pans on a set of scales. He pointed to them with a puzzled frown.

'I've heard the gods weigh men's souls,' said Asgrim incuriously. 'Perhaps that's what these pans represent. Or perhaps they're just intended to hold a lantern. They'll do for that purpose, anyway.' He took the lantern from Flügel and set it up on one of the pans, directing the beam at the slab he was about to excavate.

The pickaxe swung in the still air, a flash of polished metal in the flickering light. Steel rang sharply on stone, and a deep scar appeared across the tyrant's proud face. Asgrim lowered the pick, peeled off his leather tunic and then resumed his labour. The confines of the chamber made it stifling work. Within minutes the sweat was pouring off Asgrim's sleekly muscled skin, but he kept up an unrelenting rhythm that slowly chipped away at the slab. The pickaxe pulled back, held a moment, scythed forward and struck with a ringing jolt, scattering chips of marble – again, and again, and again. In the lamplight the barbarian looked like an oiled machine, a tireless automaton fashioned in the form of a classical athlete.

At last he paused to drink a little water. 'I could use the help of Anvil Delvanbreeks for this,' he

41

muttered, relishing the kiss of cool water on parched lips.

'Who's he?' asked Flügel.

'A dwarf I once knew. Short stature, short temper. Good at digging, though.' Asgrim did not want to pause from his work too long, as that would allow the burning in his arms to stiffen into fatigue. Taking a deep breath, he squared his shoulders and once more set about the stone. By now a deep crater had been dug out of the wall, leaving no trace of the carving. Eventually the tip of the pick broke through to the other side. Asgrim acknowledged it with just a short grunt of satisfaction, preferring to press on until the task was complete.

Sometime later a hole more than a cubit across had been hewn through the slab. Asgrim had been toiling for almost an hour. He gave an exhausted sigh and stepped back, letting the pick clatter to the ground.

'Do you want some more water?' said Flügel, holding out the bottle. He kept his eyes trained warily on the hole. The lamplight showed little but blackness beyond.

Asgrim took the bottle, but reached to hand it back when he discovered his hand was shaking too much to hold it steady. 'You'll have to hold it to my lips,' he said. 'My arms feel as heavy as lead.'

CHAPTER FOUR

 Some food and water and a short rest restored Asgrim's vigour. To Flügel's amazement, he took up his sword and swept it back and forth in fast practice strokes before dextrously returning it to its sheath with a single fluid motion.

'By Sinh, you barbarians are not mortal men!' he said. 'Anyone else would be bone-weary, yet now you seem fresh for the fray.'

'My people, the Valrings, have many foes,' said Asgrim by way of explanation. 'Fatigue is not a luxury we can afford.' He picked up his harness of studded leather and pulled it on, then went over and fetched the lantern. Shining the beam into the hole he had made, he peered through.

Flügel joined him. A tunnel led on, down into the bowels of the tomb. There were no wall paintings or carvings here. Blocks of plain stone loured greyly in the flickering light, marking the route that they had to take: the same route that Chungor Khan had taken, atop his gilded catafalque, on the journey to his final resting place.

Reaching through to set the lantern on the floor ahead of him, Asgrim disappeared into the hole. A moment later he called back to Flügel to join him. The little thief ducked through with a grace belied by his grotesquely twisted appearance, coughing slightly in the musty air. Asgrim left the lantern where it was and kindled a resin torch. It sputtered to life, giving off almost as much pungent smoke as illumination. Then he drew his sword, keeping the torch in his left hand, and moved off along the passage. Flügel picked up the lantern and followed, keeping close to the barbarian's shoulder so as to shine the light past him into the depths. If they encountered anything that Asgrim had to fight, he could not rely on the torch alone for light.

They moved on in silence for some time. It was as though the sheer antiquity of the tomb had overawed them, robbed them of speech. Or perhaps it was only that they experienced the furtiveness that all thieves feel – even those who come to steal from the dead.

The tunnel descended, stout butresses of stone supporting the roof at intervals. More carvings appeared, much simpler than those above: crude figures scratched into the hard rock walls.

'We are approaching the tomb,' said Flügel.

'You can sense it?' said Asgrim.

Flügel shook his head. 'I know these signs. Tomb builders put carvings close to the central chamber, where much excavation work is necessary. The more extravagant murals are kept for the entrance, where they are displayed for all to see. The tunnel between the tomb chamber and the entrance is usually constructed with all speed, and there's little opportunity for decoration.'

'I suspect this isn't the first tomb you've robbed,' Asgrim replied.

Flügel gave a snort. 'I've done some others. Usually they'd been broken into before I got there, the choicest items long gone. You have to come far to find an unplundered tomb like this one.'

Asgrim took another step forward, only to feel the tunnel floor give way under his weight. Instead of firm stone, he had stepped on to a platform of thin plaster that had been constructed over a deep shaft – one of the devilish traps left behind by the architects of the tomb. He flung the torch and sword forward and grabbed hold of the lip of the shaft as he fell. The impact in his arms as they caught his full weight drew a bellow of pain from his lungs, and his fingers scraped on the stone, but he held on.

The shaft did not quite reach to the walls, leaving a narrow ledge there. After edging along this, Flügel reached down and helped Asgrim clamber to safety.

Asgrim nodded as his companion handed him his sword. 'They were crafty, those tomb builders,' he said. 'And keen to guard their overlord's treasures.'

'I told you,' said Flügel: 'they feared the wrath of his ghost.'

Asgrim cast a wry glance down the pit. There was no bottom in sight. 'That would have been an unpleasant end,' he muttered. 'I might have fallen all the way to hell.'

Flügel gave a snort of bleak laughter. 'That sounds like another Norscan peculiarity: caring how you meet your death. Isn't one way just the same as another?'

Asgrim retrieved the torch and they continued along the tunnel. 'Some men seem to think that death is always bad,' he said in answer to Flügel's remark. 'Among my people life is precious, but we do not have that morbid dread of death that seems to come with civilization.'

'So I've heard,' said Flügel from behind him. 'Isn't it a great glory for you Norscans to die in battle?'

'Yes, for then the All-Father accepts our souls into his great hall beyond the rainbow. I pray he lets me face some direful tomb-guardian so that I can meet my end with sword in hand.'

'Be careful with your prayers!' said Flügel. 'Surely you do not hope for death? We have great riches to spend first.'

Asgrim shrugged his wide shoulders. 'There is not enough water on the mules for us both to reach Tarkesh Varn again. I would merely prefer a quick end in battle to a lingering death from thirst.'

There was a long pause. Flügel's voice had an odd hushed tone when he replied: 'It's true about the water. But who would know if you were to kill me, far out here in the wilderness, and return alone?'

'I would know,' said Asgrim curtly. 'A Valring warrior does not murder his comrade. I would loathe to live an hour longer if I were to commit such a betrayal.'

'Self-loathing . . .' murmured Flügel half to himself. 'That's something I know all about.' Suddenly he woke out of his reverie: 'Barbarian! Stop!'

Arriving at a low arch in the tunnel, Asgrim had bent down and was about to swing himself under using the keystone of the arch for support. He turned and looked at Flügel with a puzzled frown.

Flügel gently pulled him back and pointed to the keystone. 'It's a trap. See the groove there? The keystone's loose. If you put any weight on it, you'd dislodge it and likely the whole tunnel would cave in on us.'

Asgrim held up his torch to scrutinize the arch, then blew out a slow breath. 'You've sharp eyes, my friend.'

Flügel ducked down and shone the lantern under the arch. There was a short passage ahead, and then an open doorway. Flügel's face lit up with triumph, making him look like an ugly little doll. 'Look!' he said. He scurried eagerly forward.

Taking care to crouch low as he passed under the dangerous keystone, Asgrim followed. 'Be careful,' he warned.

But Flügel seemed not to hear him. He had become oblivious of everything but what lay ahead. For the lantern-light reflected back out of the darkness with the unmistakable glistening of gold. Greed pulled them like fish into a net.

CHAPTER FIVE

At last they had reached the burial chamber in the very heart of the tomb. Huge pillars supported the weight of stone above them. A catafalque of glimmering granite occupied the centre of the chamber, and on this lay the bones of the dead tyrant, shining with the colour of polished jade in the torchlight. Flügel played the beam of his lantern into the gloom and gave a stifled sob of avaricious joy. Gold and jewels were piled against the walls like sparkling drifts of sand.

They stepped forward into the chamber. Even Asgrim's senses reeled at the sight of such lavish wealth strewn down as carelessly as reeds that carpet the floors of a castle. His constant battle-wariness thus dimmed for a moment, he did not notice at first the rustling sound that came from the skeleton on the slab.

With dreamlike fluid grace, a glistening black serpent stirred inside the ribcage. The abrupt awareness of its presence sent an electric thrill through Asgrim's body. He spun, sword raised, to see the serpent emerging from the skull's open jaws like an obscenely long tongue.

'Another snake!' he snarled. 'I'll make short work of this one.'

'It is most unwise,' said Flügel in a voice laced with poison, 'to judge by first appearances.'

Before he could take a step, Asgrim felt a prick of steel at his back. It was a knife. 'So, you want all the treasure for yourself?' he growled. 'You are stupid as well as treacherous, Flügel – you couldn't carry a tenth of it.'

Flügel's only answer was a nervous, wicked laugh. To Asgrim's amazement, it was the serpent that replied. In a voice that thundered in his brain, all sibilant sounds and fluting vowels, it spoke to him as though across a gulf of centuries.

Asgrim's head swum. With a gasp like a drowning man, he dropped his sword and pressed his hands to his temples, fighting to make sense out of the eerie howling inside his mind. It sounded like a thousand voices screaming from the bottom of a vast well. The barbarian gave a bellow of anguish and defiance that made the stone walls ring: *'Who are you?'*

But he already knew the answer. The voice he had heard was the spirit of the dead tyrant. The living ghost of Chungor Khan.

The serpent's hypnotic eyes bored into his own, and again Asgrim thought to hear the voiceless words. They told of ancient secrets – of how the goddess Meretseger, whom the Khan had worshipped, came to him in a vision as he lay dying, promising him he would rise again a thousand years after his death. His spirit would endure in the form of a serpent that would grow inside his mouldering skeleton. When the serpent entered a living body, the Khan would be reincarnated.

'For my third and last gift, give me strength more terrible than ever before!' the Khan had pleaded of his goddess. 'Let me reconquer all my empire, and build upon it until my will knows no bounds!'

'So shall it be,' the goddess whispered. 'Your reincarnated body will have the strength of ten, a tenfold lifespan in which to wreak your deeds. Unvanquishable by mortal man or force of any weapon, now you will truly be the lord of the earth, my favourite son . . .'

And so, evilly content, the tyrant had surrendered to the dark clutch of death for a thousand years.

'But I got here first,' explained Flügel. Apparently he too could hear the serpent's telepathic voice.

Asgrim gave vent to a scornful snort. '*You*, Flügel? Past the lizards and the dragon and all the other traps?'

'Yes, that's right,' hissed Flügel, burning with anger at this mockery. 'Alone. I used my cunning to get past every obstacle and danger that you've just stormed your way through by brute force. I was useless to Chungor Khan, though: he had no desire to return to the living as a wretched cripple. So I made a deal: I'd go and bring someone else here, someone who would provide the tyrant with a fine strong body. You, you stupid barbarian!'

Asgrim reacted to this ranting speech as might be expected. His elbow shot back, driving hard into Flügel's belly. The hunchback, reactions slowed by rage, was taken by surprise. He gave a grunt and folded, collapsing to the floor.

Turning in a single motion, Asgrim snatched up the knife and spun around, hurling it towards the serpent's swaying head. His aim was true, but he had forgotten the goddess's gift. No weapon could harm the tyrant now. The dagger broke against the serpent's scales and fell harmlessly to the floor.

There was a hush in the tomb for a moment as Asgrim stood facing his eerie foe. The only sound was of Flügel softly gurgling as he struggled to draw breath.

Then Asgrim broke the silence – not with a vaunting battle-cry, but with coldly deliberate words: 'So, you sit waiting to steal another man's body, and no weapon nor mortal warrior can do you harm. You think your scheming has reached fruition, you devil-spawn? Not so! For I can carry your twisting serpentine form away from here sealed in a casket, and cast you where you can do no harm – off the eastern edge of the world, if need be! See how many people you find to prey on in the depths of the Abyss, monster!'

The serpent lifted its obsidian head and regarded Asgrim with an icily gleaming gaze. The barbarian took a pace towards it and hesitated. He could feel something stirring in the centuries-old air of the tomb. A taste of lightning soured his mouth. The hairs on the nape of his neck prickled.

Asgrim could see no immediate danger, but the harsh life of the northern highlands had taught him to trust his instincts. He crouched and picked up his sword, then slowly turned, seeking for the hidden threat that had alerted his hunter's sense.

It descended out of nowhere, slowly lowering from the empty shadows of the ceiling: a horrific sentinel summoned by Chungor Khan's magic. Under the bronze helmet there was no mortal visage, but instead a grinning skull-face from which two ghastly eyes shone like emeralds. It was no mere zombie or undead skeleton, though – Asgrim could have dealt easily enough with such a creature – for its body was formed of hard muscle the colour of clay, and eldritch red fire flickered around its fists. *Draugr* was the Norscan name for such monsters. Asgrim had heard tales of them in his childhood, on winter nights when the wind had howled under the eaves of the mead-hall. They dwelt in the cold depths of the river of death and were supposed to be unkillable.

The wound in his leg throbbed. He ignored it. Raising his sword high, he rushed forward and swung mightily towards the fleshless green-eyed face. The draugr had no weapon, but it needed none. Red sparks of plasma crawled slowly along its dead grey limbs. Lines of shining coral light coruscated around its hands as it reached to intercept Asgrim's desperate blow.

The chamber rang with the scream of metal being twisted apart. Asgrim felt a shock run through his arms, and the sword was dashed from his grasp. It flew against the wall with a sharp clang, the blade snapped in two.

The draugr gave him no time to draw his dagger. Face fixed in a macabre grin, it closed to grapple, forcing its crackling spell-charged hands heavily down on Asgrim's shoulders. Pain jolted through every fibre of the barbarian's body. He grabbed at the monster's wrists, but it was like seizing two red-hot brands. His teeth gritted and sweat started out on his brow as he struggled with swiftly failing strength. His roar of defiance sounded like the cry of a wounded bear, but all his efforts were powerless against the draugr's might. Asgrim was forced to his knees.

Pain racked his body and danced in a rose-coloured haze in front of his eyes. Still the draugr continued to press down on his shoulders, its strength flowing not only from its titanic frame but from the magical energy of its grip. Asgrim placed one hand on the floor and braced himself, but still he was bent lower and lower. It was as though a boulder were crushing down on his back. Out of the corner of his eye he saw the black serpent. It had slithered down from the catafalque and was moving closer, ready to enter his mouth and possess his body for itself.

The agony began to recede as a shadow seemed to settle over him, and he realized he had reached the last dregs of his endurance. Unconsciousness would swiftly be followed by death. Fouler still would it be to live again, but now possessed by the vile twisted soul of the tyrant . . .

A memory flashed into his mind – one of the songs the skald had sung to the warriors of his clan. It concerned a bygone time of heroes, when valiant defenders had begun to weaken in the face of marauding onslaughts. The skald, depicting the last few defenders of the hall, had recited their lord's exhortation to them to sell their lives dearly. Asgrim heard the skald's words again – an instant flashing out of all the memories of his life. They had not lost their power to stir him: *'Resolve must be harder, heart the keener, courage the greater, as our might lessens!'*

Asgrim had always relied on his battle skills, but against the unhuman draugr they were of no avail. Now he was forced back on raw courage. A sword could be broken, a spear knocked aside, a shield split – they were unreliable weapons. But a Norscan warrior always had his courage.

Despite the pain of the draugr's fiery grasp, Asgrim gave a great shout and heaved with every vestige of his strength. Incredibly, the draugr could not stop him from getting up on to one knee. The other leg, planted firmly now, thrust upwards as Asgrim locked his arms around his foe.

And so they stood, grappling, two statues of indomitable strength, neither able to gain the advantage. Living defiance battled with the clay-cold rigidity of death. Fierce barbarian blood-lust stared back at an icy emerald gaze.

For all his spirit, Asgrim could not have kept up this struggle for long. But he did not have to. Instead of a battle between himself and the draugr, it had become a contest of endurance matching his bravery against Chungor Khan's magic. Deep in the cold brain of the serpent, realization stirred: the magic that had summoned the draugr could not be maintained. The barbarian's will was too strong. The serpent veered away across the stone floor, forgetting the battle, seeing one last hope for victory . . .

As the spell that had summoned it lapsed, the draugr vanished like a nightmare on waking, disappearing back into the realm of shadow from which it had come. Asgrim gave a groan of pain and reeled back. His reprieve had come not a moment too soon. Another heartbeat – half a heartbeat – and he would have fallen.

But the battle was not yet won. Not while the serpent carrying Chungor Khan's soul was loose in the world. Still staggering from his ordeal, he shook his head to clear it and looked around.

The serpent glided across the floor to where Flügel lay gasping. Before Asgrim could move, it had slithered into his mouth.

Startled, Flügel jerked frantically to his knees, his eyes bulging in shock. He tried to cry out, but his voice was choked off by the loathsome worm that was sliding down his throat. As its tail disappeared into his mouth, Flügel made a retching noise and raised his hands towards his former comrade. 'Asgrim,' he pleaded in a voice weak with fear, 'help me . . .'

Flügel had proved a treacherous colleague, but it gave Asgrim no glee to see him suffer so awful a fate. 'There's nothing I can do,' he said grimly.

Flügel's body suddenly went into spasms. Veins pulsed like wriggling snakes under his skin. He hugged himself – a frightened child, grotesque face contorted into a drained white mask of abject terror. 'I can feel it inside me,' he wailed. 'Merciful gods! *It's eating my soul . . . !*'

His long shrill scream echoed off the cold stone walls. Then abruptly there was silence. Flügel's head slumped forward like a puppet with its strings cut.

Asgrim watched him for a moment, but there was no movement. He might have been dead. Asgrim sensed gathering danger. He crept forward, cat-like, and picked up the broken sword.

His eyes flicked off the motionless hunchback for just a split second. When he looked back, Flügel had lifted his head and was staring straight at him. No, not Flügel any more. Chungor Khan.

The lopsided body lurched to its feet. As Chungor Khan sucked in his first breath in ten centuries, he made a noise low in his throat, somewhere between a sigh and a growl. He kept a hard glare fixed on Asgrim as his tongue strove to form words:

'I live again,' he said. Where Flügel's voice had been merely bitter, his was acid with evil.

He glanced at his twisted limbs, then regarded the barbarian with hooded eyes. Asgrim felt as if he were in the presence of a human snake. 'You chose to reject the honour I offered you, of providing me with my new body,' the Khan said. 'And so you have doomed me to live out my long second life in this skewed carcass.'

'Now your outward appearance reflects the putridity of your black heart,' replied Asgrim, waving his sword from side to side as he advanced like a snake-charmer waving his pipe.

Chungor Khan seemed unconcerned by either the taunt or the weapon. 'A part of the thief's soul still lives within me,' he said. 'I sense his bitterness; I shall make it mine. Since I have been forced to clothe myself in this twisted lump of flesh, I shall revenge myself on all mankind. Now I will go forth from my resting-place and once more impose my rule upon the lands of men, and the deeds I'll do will be the very terrors of the world. I shall make each day a monument to hatred; rivers of blood will flow to fill the altar-cups of my goddess. The wars of your era will seem as the tantrums of children beside the carnage I shall wreak!'

Asgrim acknowledged all this with a feral smile. 'You're getting ahead of yourself, tyrant,' he said. 'You won't be leaving this tomb alive.'

Chungor Khan snarled back in fury: 'Preposterous! You have understood nothing. I am invincible; no weapon has the power to harm me, no living man can cast me down. The goddess has gifted me with the strength of ten men – enough to snap your bones like dry twigs, barbarian.'

'Then do it,' said Asgrim. Suddenly, instead of lunging to strike with the broken blade, he flung it underarm at the tyrant's face. His foe flinched back instinctively, throwing up his hands, forgetting that the weapon could not hurt him. It bounced aside and the Khan lashed out, but Asgrim had already jumped back. Snatching up the tyrant's crown from among the scattered treasure, he darted out of the chamber.

Chungor Khan's fury found its voice in a howl that rumbled up the walls of the tunnel behind Asgrim. 'Flee, then!' he screeched. 'Where will you run? I'll follow you across the wasteland like the shadow of death.'

Asgrim paused at the trapped keystone and looked back along the tunnel. Chungor Khan came hobbling towards him out of the gloom, eyes shining with malignance. Asgrim held up the crown as bait. The tyrant, seeing it, gave a horrible cry and came rushing forward.

Asgrim struck the keystone with all his strength. There was a rumbling in the rock, and he wasted no time waiting to survey the result of his action. As he turned to run, he caught a last glimpse of the tyrant flailing amidst falling rubble. On Flügel's crooked legs and club foot, he could not move fast enough to get clear. If he had any last curse to hurl at Asgrim's retreating back, it was lost in the roar of the collapsing tunnel.

Asgrim ran for his life. Pain stabbed through his wounded thigh, the bandage binding it soaked in blood from his exertions, but he ignored it. His breath came in hot agonized gasps and his legs pumped furiously, oblivious of fatigue. Everything had been stripped away now – might, courage, cunning, even naked determination. He was like a wild animal in whom only the instinct of survival remained. With every last vestige of his strength, he raced on through darkness as the tomb caved in behind him.

At last he saw the flash of daylight ahead and hurled himself through to sprawl on the hot gravel in front of the tomb. Stone dust gusted out of the passage behind him and then the heavy stone lintel fell with a crump, blocking the entrance for ever.

For a long time Asgrim lay there stretched before the tomb as consciousness slowly seeped back. Finally, realizing the sun would bake him dry if he did not move, he dragged himself under the shade of the columns and clawed down a bottle from one of the pack-mules. The water was warm and tasteless, but the shock of it in his parched throat restored Asgrim's senses. He sat up and saw that he still held the gold crown: the single treasure he had managed to take from the tyrant's tomb.

The crown was a heavy gold circlet set with one large limpid green jewel. As Asgrim gazed numbly at it, he seemed to discern a flicker of sinuous movement in the depths of the jewel. Swimming into focus came the face of a snake-tongued woman. Asgrim was transfixed in awe, for this was the face of the goddess. Her coldly burning eyes held his. He heard a voice of languid beauty, terrible and alluring, that promised untold riches and power if he would agree to serve her as the tyrant had . . .

It seemed for an instant as though the band of the crown had become the coils of a golden snake, encircling Asgrim's wrist with a light caress. He hurled it away with a cry of revulsion. It struck one of the pillars of the colonnade and rolled out into the dusty sunlight – now just a dented artifact of gold, the insidious jewel cracked and clouded.

Asgrim sat back against the wall of the tomb and pushed himself upright. A glance at the collapsed entrance-way told him that the tyrant would never emerge to trouble the world with his evil. Even the strength of a hundred men could not have freed him from under those colossal blocks of masonry. Asgrim felt a twinge of pity for Flügel. He had duped the barbarian in an evil plan that had nearly cost Asgrim his very soul, but now he hoped that Flügel was at peace. The little hunchback's life had been filled with misery enough; in death he should be free of cares.

With weary steps Asgrim led the mules away. Resolving in future to seek more wholesome treasure – treasure bearing no curse, and safe to spend – he began the long trek homeward . . .

THE END

A GROWL OF THUNDER

A Solitaire Quest for a Barbarian

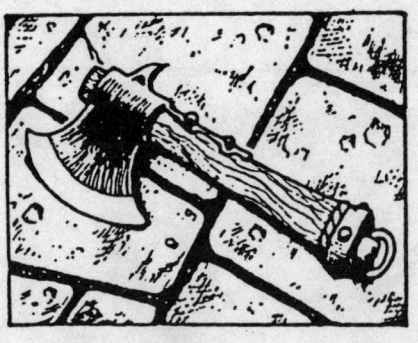

A GROWL OF THUNDER

This is a HeroQuest adventure for which you will require the HeroQuest board game. You will need a GamesMaster and just one player. Rules are the same as for any HeroQuest game, but the adventure has one difference: it is only for a Barbarian. Just one Barbarian at a time may try his luck at this quest. If other players wish to tackle it, they must wait their turn.

The description of the adventure begins over the page. DO NOT READ THE FOLLOWING SEVEN PAGES UNLESS YOU INTEND TO GAMESMASTER THIS ADVENTURE. (If no GamesMaster is available, go straight to the solo gamebook adventure on page 71.)

THE ADVENTURE
(GamesMaster Only)

Read this to the player:

You have travelled far and wide, seeking adventure in all corners of the world. But it is always the wild heaths and tangled pine forests of your Norscan land where you are really at home.

One day, returning to visit your tribe, you are alarmed by a smell of wood-smoke in the cold air. Hurrying over the next bluff, your worst fears are confirmed: the great stave-hall of your people is engulfed in flames!

You race to the hall and help your clan-cousins drag survivors out of the burning wreckage. Old Thidrand, your father's steward, stands coughing. He is blackened in soot and his face is raw with burns, but he is trying to get back into the burning hall. 'The lord is still in there!' he wails.

You dive through the doors without hesitation and battle through the heat and smoke until you catch sight of your father, Lord Thunrir. He is pinned by a smouldering timber beam that has fallen across his legs. With every ounce of strength, you heft the beam up and drag him clear. Straight away you can see that he is not long for this world. Gazing up at you with stern eyes, he says, 'It was the orcs of Stalac Tor. They attacked without warning, having used fell sorcery to blind our sentries. You must avenge your people — and more than that, you must recover the three sacred treasures of the Thunder God which the orcs have stolen!'

Those are his last words in this world. You waste no time on lamentation. Leaving the women and the wounded to bury the dead, you take up your weapons and set out across the moors to the ancient mound where the orcs have their lair. Soon you see it looming ahead. The wind whips your cloak behind you, making you look like an avenging demon in the blood-drenched sunset.

You stride towards the mound . . .

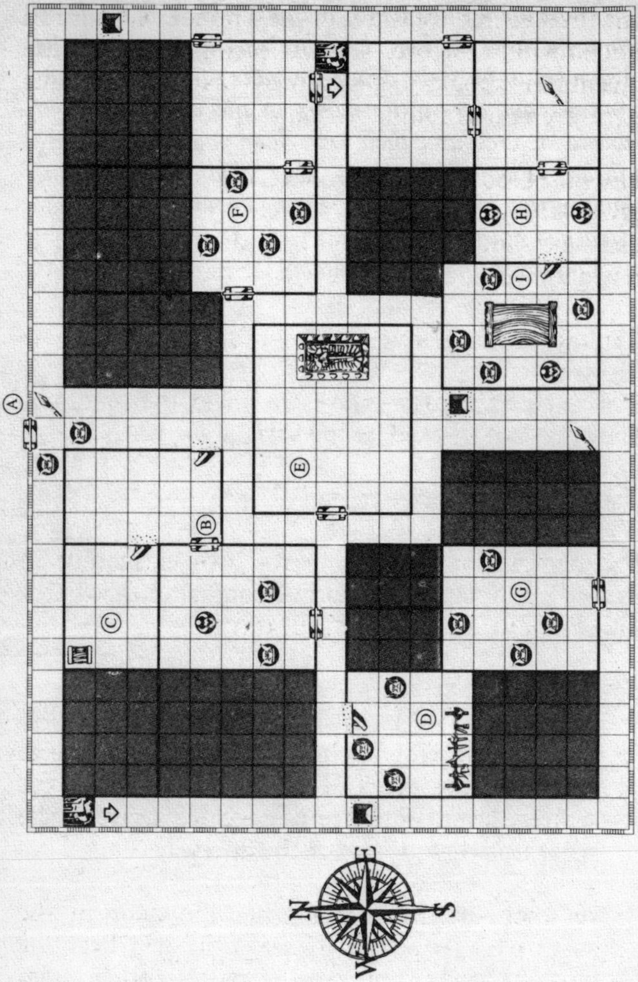

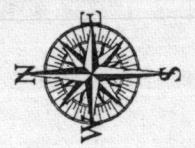

The three sacred treasures of the Thunder God are all hidden within the orcs' lair. As each is retrieved, the adventurer should be informed that he/she gains extra strength in combat as follows:

Thunder God's Belt (see room C)
ARMOUR
The belt allows you to roll four dice in defence. It may not be used by the Wizard.

Thunder God's Gloves (see room D)
ARMOUR
You must have these gloves to wield the hammer. They may not be used by the Wizard.

Hammer of Thor (see room I)
WEAPON
The hammer allows you to roll two extra dice in attack. It can be used in normal combat or thrown (it will return to you for use the next turn).

Enter at A

A: In the north side of the mound is the door that leads into the orcs' lair. Note that the two orc sentries in the entrance passage are aware of the spear trap directly beside the doorway.

B: As the Barbarian approaches the door in the south-west corner of the room he will hear the guttural speech of orcs from the other side, answered by a deep voice which rings with an eerie metallic echo.

C: The chest here contains a magical belt with a buckle in the shape of a thunderbolt. This is the first of the three stolen treasures of the Thunder God. Anyone wearing it gets to roll twice as many dice in defence.

D: These three goblins are part of the retinue of Balor (see room I) and have been told to wait here while he consults with the orc chieftains. They are guarding the weapons rack, which contains the second of the stolen treasures: the Thunder God's gloves.

E: This is the central chamber of the mound, which was originally the burial mound of Grashlŷg, an ancient orc warlord. The orcs know better than to enter this chamber, since the act of opening the door will awaken Grashlŷg as an undead wight (use the mummy figure):

Move 4 squares
Attack 4 dice
Defend 4 dice

Body ▢▢▢☠

Mind 3

Once awake, Grashlŷg will stalk through the mound attacking anyone who gets in his path – friend or foe!

F: These four orcs are savagely beating a human Wizard whom they've captured. If the Barbarian keeps the orcs busy for three consecutive turns, this gives the Wizard a chance to recover and join in. This Wizard (whose name is Balash) has already used some spells but still has those of Water and Earth. He has the normal attribute values of a player wizard.

G: This is where the orcs sleep, and these four are slumbering contentedly having just returned from torching the stave-hall of the Barbarian's tribe. Each needs to roll a six at the start of their turn to wake up, or will wake up instantly if attacked. (Their clothing still smells of smoke and there is dried human blood on their axes, so the Barbarian should be in no doubt what they've been up to.)

H: These two Chaos warriors are the honour guard of Balor the Chaos sorcerer, and bear his personal coat-of-arms on their shields: four serpents intertwining to form an eight-pointed star.

I: Balor the Chaos sorcerer is deep in discussion with the elders of the orc tribe. On the table in front of them is Thor's Hammer, the third of the stolen treasures. The orcs summoned Balor here to give him the hammer (hopefully for a lavish reward of gold) so that he could take it back to his dread master Morcar. But they have a problem: no-one has been able to move the hammer since it was brought back here.

What they haven't yet realized is that only someone wearing the Thunder God's gloves (room D) can lift the hammer. If the Barbarian has these, he will be able to snatch up the hammer and use it himself. As soon as he does this, sparks of lightning shoot from the hammer to strike the orcs, killing them instantly. Balor, though, is made of sterner stuff:

Move 7 squares
Attack 5 dice
Defend 4 dice

Body ▢▢▢☠

Mind 4

Wrap-up

The Barbarian returns to his tribe with the three sacred treasures. Nothing can restore the slain to life, but at least they can rest with honour now. The Barbarian is the new chieftain, and under his direction the task of rebuilding the hall begins . . .

THE TREASURE OF CHUNGOR KHAN

A Solo Adventure for a Barbarian

THE TREASURE OF CHUNGOR KHAN

This is a solo adventure for a barbarian. All you will need are a paper, pencil and a normal six-sided dice.

You are about to set out on an intriguing quest. In it you will discover what would have happened if *you*, not Asgrim, had sought the tyrant's tomb. A word of warning: you are not as tough a fighter as Asgrim, so you will need to use your wits as well as your sword. Also, some of the obstacles you must face will be different from those in the story. That is the nature of Chaos. You might need to make several attempts before you succeed, but persevere and perhaps you will win for yourself the title of Hero.

Now read the rules, and then you will be ready to set out . . .

RULES OF THE ADVENTURE

Characteristics
You have four characteristics:

BODY measures the amount of physical injury you can endure. Keep track of your BODY score, which will vary as you are wounded. If BODY is ever reduced to zero, you are dead. Lost BODY points can be healed by magical means, but no spell or item will ever take your BODY score above its initial level.

MIND represents your mental and psychic resilience. This characteristic measures your resistance to hostile sorcery. Keep track of your MIND score; if it ever reaches zero this means you have literally died of shock.

COMBAT indicates your ability to fight. This usually remains the same throughout the adventure, but can be changed if you lose a weapon – or gain a better one, perhaps. Having your COMBAT score reduced to zero is unlikely to occur, and does *not* indicate death.

SPEED is an indicator of dexterity and reflexes as well as movement rate. If your SPEED is reduced to zero you have been immobilized and must abandon your quest.

Initial values for each of the four characteristics are

already given on the Character Sheet on page 77. Permission is granted for you to photocopy this Character Sheet for your use while playing *The Treasure of Chungor Khan*.

Fighting

When you fight an opponent, the battle is considered to take place in *rounds*. Every round, you get an attempt to strike an opponent whom you're fighting. To do so, you must roll *equal to or less than* your COMBAT score on one dice. (For instance, if you have a COMBAT score of 4 then you'll need to roll 1–4 on the dice to hit your foe.)

If you succeed in scoring a hit, this inflicts the loss of one BODY point. Your enemy will also get the chance each round to strike back at you, of course (you must roll the dice for them), and any blow that they land will cost *you* one BODY point.

Remember that if a character's BODY points are reduced to zero, the character is killed.

Multiple opponents

When you encounter a *group* of foes, all of them will get a chance to hit you every round. But, regardless of how many opponents you are fighting, you yourself can only make *one* COMBAT roll per round. This means that multiple opponents are very deadly, and you must be careful.

Parrying

Instead of attacking in any given round, you can try to parry. You must decide this at the very start of the round, before rolling the dice for any of the attacks for that round. You *must* have a weapon in order to parry.

To parry, you need to roll 1 or 2 on the dice. A successful parry negates *one* blow struck against you in that round.

Monsters do not parry.

Fleeing

Sometimes you will be given the option of fleeing from a battle. This might not seem exactly heroic – but discretion is sometimes the better part of valour, and by retreating you might even find a better place to make a stand.

If you choose to flee, try to roll your SPEED or less on one dice. Failure means that you lose one BODY point before getting away; success means you manage to escape unscathed.

Encumbrance

You can carry a maximum of six items at one time. If you come across an item when you are already at your limit, you will have to discard something to make room for it. Note that you start off with a sword, and if this is lost you must deduct one point from COMBAT until you find another weapon to replace it.

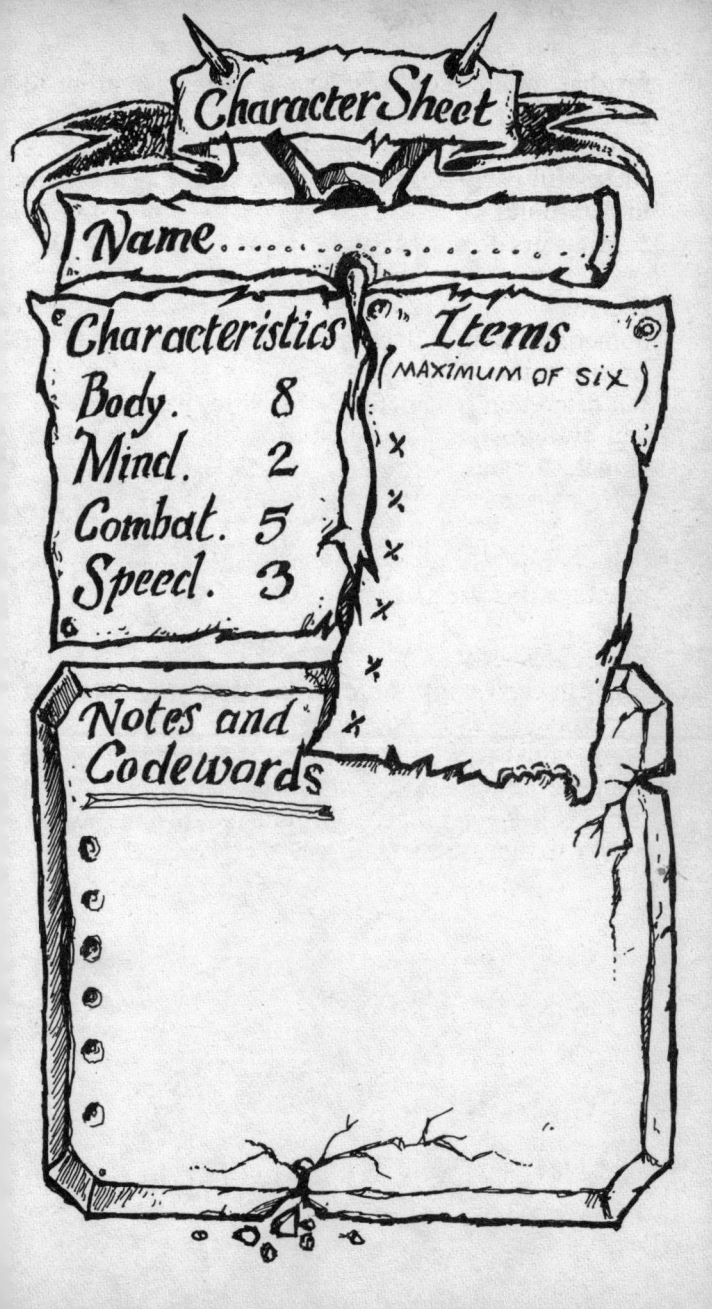

Character Sheet

Name ....

Characteristics

Body.   8
Mind.   2
Combat.   5
Speed.   3

Items
(MAXIMUM OF SIX)

x
x
x
x
x
x

Notes and Codewords

1

Begin by writing the items you are carrying on your Character Sheet. You have a sword, a bow and a money-pouch containing ten silver pieces. (The money-pouch only counts as a single item, no matter how many coins it contains.)

You are in one of the many foetid taverns of Rune-port, a wretchedly isolated town on the southern coast of Charlisoix – or 'Charlie's Socks' as the native non-Brettonians mockingly call it. You came here in search of adventure, but the most adventure you have had so far is in avoiding the rats, pickpockets and drunken gangs of off-duty soldiers that infest the narrow cobbled streets.

'So that's the map, eh?'

'Yeah. 'E didn't want to part wiv it. 'Ad to take a few of 'is fingers as well.'

'Wondered what the red smudge was.'

You look up, intrigued by this snippet of obviously villainous conversation. At the next table sit two small furtive-looking men with three ears, seven scars and an eyepatch between the two of them. They are bent over a torn scrap of parchment.

If you approach them to find out what they're up to, turn to **25**

If you eavesdrop for a bit longer, turn to **39**

If you go to the bar to get yourself another drink, turn to **53**

2

You begin your ascent of Mount Kringla, hefting yourself up its huge rocky flanks, fingers grasping hard at each small crack. As you climb, you glance into the depths of the sky where storm clouds are massing. You must pray to your wild Norscan gods that the blizzard holds off until you have reached the summit, since the icy breath of a snowstorm would soon dislodge you and send you tumbling down to be shattered on the distant rocks below.

Roll one dice.

If you score less than or equal to your SPEED, turn to **70**

If you score greater than your SPEED, turn to **8**

3

You can swim no further. Down you drift, lungs filling with icy water. It is like being in a dream. Peaceful and dark, here beneath the raging waves. So silent.

Others arrived here before you. Other mariners shipwrecked in days gone by. They welcome you now with coral embrace, pearl eyes gleaming at the newcomer in their midst. They smile their fixed white smiles and watch you find your place on the sea bed beside them.

Darkness descends. Your last thought is that you did not die in battle, as a Norscan should. You will descend into oblivion for all time, never to enjoy the pleasures of the All-Father's mead hall. The thought stirs a momentary stab of panic, but it is no more than a distant and tiny voice, and soon it too is silent and there is nothing to disturb the peace of the ocean depths.

4

Night has long fallen by the time you reach the other side of the mere. Fetching armfuls of reeds, you fashion a bed and settle down for the night.

The reeds are damp and stink of river-mud, and the coldness of the place keeps you awake. Just as you are dropping into a fretful doze, the soft crack of a damp twig jerks you to your feet. Breath indrawn, sword in your hand, you are reacting on instinct as an indistinct shape bursts out of the undergrowth to attack you.

UNKNOWN ASSAILANT   COMBAT 3   BODY ?

Fight on as best you can, but you must deduct one COMBAT point for this battle because you are in pitch darkness.

Fleeing is out of the question.

If you manage to inflict a total of three BODY points on your mysterious foe, turn to **124**

5
This is the magical weapon Propugnator. It only strikes for normal damage, but is superb in defence. When you use it to parry, you need a roll of 1–5, instead of the usual 1–2, on one dice.

If you took other items as well, turn to the relevant sections to discover what they do. If you are now ready to return to where you left the punt moored, turn to **16** if you have the codeword PSALMS

If you have the codeword CHARON, turn to **31**

6
The guards strip you of your weapons and money (cross them off your Character Sheet) but do not bother to take any other items you may possess. Then they lead you through a maze of passageways

whose walls of rough-hewn stone are blackened under centuries of grime. As you pass the heavy iron-barred doorways on your route, you hear the moans and pitiful shrieks of other inmates. 'That's how you'll sound, after a few years in this place,' remarks one of the guards. 'Madness is the only escape from here.'

Shoving you roughly into a small cell, they slam the door. The scrape of the key in the lock makes a doleful sound in the gloomy cell.

One of the guards slides open a panel in the door and sneers: 'Don't bother getting comfortable. You won't be here that long.'

The panel bangs shut and you listen to their footfalls recede along the corridor outside. Apart from the rats snuffling about in the corners of the cell, you are alone.

Then the full horror of your predicament falls on you like ice water. They mean to execute you for a crime you did not commit! You must escape.

If you have the Cloth of Marvels, turn to **152**

Otherwise, turn to **19**

7

The battle is short but furious. With the guards dead, you can now take the bunch of keys and also the bow if you wish. Note them on your Character Sheet if you do.

If you have not already done so, and now want to use the keys to unlock the cell next door to the guardroom, turn to **87**

If you decide to carry on to the end of the passage to look for a way out, turn to **102**

Your foot slips on a slick patch of ice that has formed on one of the ledges. With a scream, you plummet back down the mountainside, returning in seconds along a route which took you hours to ascend.

Death seems inevitable, but suddenly you are caught by powerful arms and borne up again towards the heavens. You can hardly believe your eyes as, turning to see what has got hold of you, you behold a lovely gold-haired woman astride a pale horse.

'You're a Valkyrie!' you breathe in astonishment.

She smiles, staying silent. Just as well: only the dead hear a Valkyrie's sweet words of comfort.

The Valkyrie spurs her horse down until its hooves touch on the windswept snows of the mountain peak. Her slender arm looks scarcely strong enough to hold a full pitcher of mead, yet she handles you as a mortal maid would heft a kitten, setting you down beside the horse. Then, turning her eyes upwards to the wide snow-laden heavens, she digs her white heels into the horse's flanks and it goes soaring up into the air. You watch until a crack of sunlight, penetrating the black blanket of cloud, causes a brilliant rainbow to shine momentarily across the darkening sky.

You shake your head, stunned. It is unknown for the Valkyries to interfere in mortal matters. Their only task is to choose the most valiant from among the slain after a battle, bearing those souls to eternal afterlife in Valhalla. That one rescued you indicates you have been selected for a great destiny. Proudly you vow to be true to that destiny: you will succeed in your quest, or die in the attempt.

You can increase your MIND score by two points, since you now have the fixity of purpose born of knowing that the great gods themselves have taken an interest in your adventure. (If you had the codeword PSALMS then delete it, as your companions were left to fall to their doom.)

Now turn to **70**

9

The next morning you set out early, travelling on through territory that becomes increasingly barren and dusty. Trees gradually disappear, giving way to coarse scrub and dry brown grass. The sunlight slants past weathered crags, dazzling but unwarming. Carrion birds wheel overhead uttering parched croaks.

Turn to **188**

10

It is hard work chipping through the door, but at least you are cheered up by the fact that this is the last exertion you will have to make. After all your perilous adventures, narrow scrapes, hair-raising encounters and hard work, at last you are on the verge of achieving your goal. Soon the tyrant's treasure will be yours!

After an hour you have smashed a hole large enough to squeeze through. You lower the axe, arms shaking with exhaustion. You must reduce your COMBAT score by one point, owing to fatigue.

Blood quickening with excitement, you duck down and enter the tomb chamber. Turn to **119**

11

You give a wild howl of laughter which astonishes them. 'But 'ow about you?' says Grinch. 'Aren't you put off by the curse?'

'We Norsemen revere *true* gods – harsh, uncompromising, uncaring monsters every one. As long as we die in battle, we are guaranteed a place in the mead hall of Eerg the All-Father, God of the Slain. I pity this snake goddess if she cares to dispute possession of my soul with grim Eerg!'

Spoken like a true barbarian warrior. Now you must back up your words with bold action. Note the codeword PSALMS on your character sheet and then turn to **156**

12

Will you:

Draw your sword and charge?   Turn to **68**
Or unlimber your bow?   Turn to **82**

13

'Oh . . . what be you doin' there?'

You turn your head, spitting out a mouthful of salt-caked sand, and look up. You must have blacked out, but the waves washed you up on to the beach. A lobsterman with a wickerwork pot in each hand is gazing down at you with an expression of blank amazement. 'Crawled out the sea, 'ave you?' he says.

You sit up, coughing. 'A wonder I didn't swallow half of it! I was jumping ship . . . the *Heldrasir* . . .'

He makes the sign of the sea god and mutters a prayer. 'The *Heldrasir*! 'Tis said she's a devil ship, doomed to sail the seas till the end o' time. An' no greater devil than her captain, Athscar, who used to be the bully-boy of the Khan centuries ago.'

'You're well informed for a lobsterman,' you say, staggering to your feet.

'Got to keep your wits about you, in the lobstering

profession.' He gives you his arm and helps you up the beach towards his hut. ''Spect you'll want to be out of those wet things.'

The map! You fumble inside your jerkin for it. Roll one dice. On a score of 1–2 you are lucky, it is still legible: turn to **28**. On a score of 3 or more, the water has made it completely unreadable and your adventure can go no further.

14

After debating the matter, you reduce his fee to three silver pieces. Cross this off, then turn to **175**

15

You leap into the punt with the satyr in hot pursuit. But Fournil is so frightened by the sight of the huge goat-legged beast that erupts out of the undergrowth that he drops the punt pole. While he scrabbles to retrieve it, you must fight to prevent your foe from getting aboard the boat.

You should have a record of the satyr's COMBAT and BODY scores. Continue your battle, and if you win turn to **49**

16

The punt is gone. You can just make it out, far off in the dusk, heading rapidly towards the far shore of the lake.

The map—! You feel inside your jerkin, but it has been removed. (Delete it from the list of items you're carrying.) You've been robbed, and you never felt a thing!

Hearing your bellow of rage, Grinch and Grivois peer back at the island and rock with laughter. The little beggars. You'd dearly like to make them pay for their villainy, if only you could get your hands on their grubby necks.

Maybe you can – you're a strong swimmer. It would mean abandoning all your belongings, but you might be able to catch up with them.

If you try that, turn to **45**

If you have a bow and want to shoot at them, turn to **59**

17

She nods, smiling, and touches your sword. 'When next you wield this sword you will instantly slay your foe. But I warn you, warrior, the spell will be broken once you've used it – so do not be too hasty to draw your blade for battle if it is not necessary.'

With those words she departs, sinking back into the impenetrable darkness of the lake. Note the enchantment she's placed on your sword: in the next fight you use it, *and for that fight only*, you will automatically win without needing to roll dice. (You might want to save your sword until you get into a really tough fight, using your bare hands for combat in the meantime. But remember that if you do that you must reduce your COMBAT score temporarily by one point.)

Making yourself a bed of reeds, you pass an uncomfortable night and arise early, eager to be on your way. Delete the codeword PSALMS and then turn to **111**

18

The guards barely glance at you as you walk past them through the gate. You emerge from the fort into the street. Free at last! Hurrying off into the town, you begin to think of the preparations you must make for crossing the desert.

Turn to **79**

19

You languish in the dank cell for several hours. Although you cannot think of a way to escape, still your mind is awhirl and sleep will not come. Late in the evening, the panel in the door slides open. You are on your feet in a trice. Is the end to come so soon? But it is only your gaoler. He grins at you, displaying rheumy gums and cracked teeth. 'Here's your supper,' he says, pushing a bowl of gruel at you between the bars.

'But it's nearly midnight,' you reply.

'I've been busy,' he grunts. 'Lodge a complaint with the management if you don't like the service.'

With a jeering laugh he departs, but you don't bother to hurl insults after him. Your attention has been caught by the metal spoon in your bowl of gruel. You glance at the stone blocks of the wall. The mortar is old. Crumbling. It will be arduous work, but it is your only hope. You set to work with the spoon.

Turn to **191**

20

You spin round and sprint along the passage. Behind you, the guards pour through the open doorway with shouts of rage.

If you did not take the bow from the weapons rack, turn to **161**

If you did take the bow, turn to **34**

21

Roll a dice and halve the score, rounding fractions up. This is the number of BODY points you lose owing to the cold. (For instance, if you rolled a 5 that would mean you lost three BODY points, and so on.)

If you survive, you stagger down out of the pass and spend an uncomfortable night sleeping rough before continuing on your way the next morning.

Turn to **111**

You find a convenient place to sleep beside a small brook. There is an old treestump nearby which you break up for firewood. Uprooting handfuls of moss to form a makeshift bed, you settle down for the night.

You are awakened as the moon is close to setting. Silver light sparkles on the grass, and the brook makes a noise like a crystal harp. You look up. Beside you stands an elfin knight in golden armour, a look of darkness in his silver eyes.

You're on your feet in an instant. Elves can be tricky to deal with. You watch him warily, waiting for him to speak.

'You owe me,' he says, 'for what you've taken.'

You scowl, puzzled. 'I took nothing of yours.'

He nods towards the ground behind you. 'My cloak? My horse's saddle? You consider these things of no account?'

You cast a careful glance backwards. Bizarrely, the moss you tore up to make your bed now appears to be a gorgeous ermine robe; the firewood is in fact a smouldering gold-chased saddle.

Frank amazement shows in your face as you give a shrug. 'I didn't know . . .'

The elfin knight studies his nails and sighs. 'No matter, if you'll pay for what you've taken. I'll accept thirteen pieces of silver.'

If you pay him the money, cross it off and turn to **36**

If you refuse (or cannot afford it) then turn to **50**

23

You stumble on throughout the day, ignoring the sweat that streams into your eyes and cakes the desert dust on your skin. At last, close to sunset, you catch sight of the detestable pair a short distance ahead of you. Uttering a vengeful roar, you race across the sand towards them.

'Lummee!' says Grinch, looking back. 'It's the barbell again, mate.'

'So it is,' says Grivois, drawing his dagger. 'Did I ever show you my recipe for Norscan fricasse . . . ?'

GRINCH	COMBAT 4	BODY 3
GRIVOIS	COMBAT 4	BODY 3

You will have to reduce your COMBAT score by one point (just for this fight) because you are worn out after chasing them so hard all day.

Nothing would induce you to flee; you desire their deaths too much for that! If you defeat them, you can retrieve the map and also take their water flask if you want it. Then turn to **164**

A sixth sense alerts you of danger just in time. Whirling, you see a skull-faced warrior dropping out of nowhere to attack you. Its clay-coloured flesh crackles with cold red fire.

The discarnate tyrant has summoned a terrible *draugr* with his necromancy. As you confront the sunken gaze and fleshless grin, you feel cold terror gnawing at your heart. It is said that the *draugr*, having died once already, are unkillable in battle. You must prove that legend wrong if you can . . .

DRAUGR   COMBAT 6   BODY 8

If you win, turn to **38**

25

You loom over the table where the weird pair are sitting. They look up, greeting you in unison with a cry of 'Beat it, you big barbarian buffoon.'

Now that is not polite.

If you decide to teach the two rogues a lesson in manners, turn to **80**

If you *insist* on joining them, turn to **93**

If you'd rather go off and seek adventure (and treasure) elsewhere, turn to **66**

You scour the stalls of the market-place, finally narrowing down your selection to just a few choice items that could come in handy during the trip:

A water flask	costs 2 silver pieces
A jar of healing salve	costs 17 silver pieces

A silver arrow	costs 10 silver pieces
A sprig of garlic	costs 1 silver piece
A lantern	costs 1 silver piece

(The healing salve will restore one lost BODY point when used; there is enough in the jar for three uses.)

Having made your purchases and crossed off the money, turn to **40**

27

You soon realize that you are not alone in being dissatisfied with the situation. Many of the crew slope around the deck casting sour looks at the captain and his officers. But when you try to see if you can stir them to mutiny, you discover it is hopeless. They are too drained of spirit, their outpourings of malcontent revealing a deep and dreamlike melancholy. 'How long have we toiled aboard this ship?' says one. 'It seems I can never remember a time when we did not. Sleet and salt-spray have roughened my skin and high waves battered me, with only a tot of rum now and again for comfort.'

'The captain will never put in at any port in the waking world,' mutters another. 'He was a loyal henchman of the Khan, and now that tyrant's dead there are many as would rip out his putrid guts and hang 'em from the yardarm. I'd like to myself, if it comes to that.'

'Then rise up against him!' you urge them. 'Mutiny. I'll help you.'

They shake their heads forlornly. 'We'd be clapped in irons,' they say. 'Hauled under the keel and told to scrape the barnacles off with our teeth. It's hopeless.'

If you have the codeword PSALMS, turn to **109**

If not, your only recourse is to try swimming back to shore: turn to **167**

28

After drying your clothes, you thank the lobsterman and go to set out on your journey. He shows you to a path that leads back up to the clifftops. Watching you go, he suddenly calls after you, 'If you're off on some big adventure, wouldn't you want to get yourself a bit of magical help first?'

If you ask him if there's anything he could suggest, turn to **174**

If you cannot be bothered to listen to any more of his wittering, turn to **147**

29

You draw your sword. 'Alone in this wild watery waste, who is to stop me taking the punt?' you ask with a crooked grin.

The young man is outraged. 'Stop!' he cries as you stride over to his punt. 'You are nothing but a common thief!'

You give a short laugh as you cast off. 'You call *me* a thief, and yet you're the one who swindles poor wayfarers out of their hard-won coinage.'

He stands at the lakeside and watches you punt off into the gathering twilight. 'Thief!' comes his voice across the water. 'Barbarian!'

You shake your head. You've been called worse things by better people. Then, turning to the west, you see the cold light of the declining sun glint off the water. A clump of tangled shadow marks out a reed-fringed island in the centre of the mere.

If you wish to stop off at the island, turn to **43**
If not, turn to **4**

30

You leap into the punt and lose no time pushing off from the shore. Not a moment too soon. As you punt rapidly away, the satyr emerges from the undergrowth to bluster at you. 'Come back, you mortal mouse!' he rages. 'Afraid to face my fury? You worm! You lubber! You frightened hare!'

'Got your goat, did I?' you shout back to taunt him. 'Go squat in your thicket, hairy-breeks!'

His replies, most probably unprintable, are swallowed up by the distance as you punt on towards the far edge of the mere.

Turn to **4**

31

Seeing you emerge from the thickets, Fournil stares at you with a face drained of colour. 'What happened?' he says in a small nervous voice. 'I heard such hideous sounds of battle, I thought you had been assailed by the Dark One himself!'

You laugh and slap him heartily on the back as you climb aboard. 'Hardly that, my friend, but it was a hard fight just the same. Come, I am weary. Punt us back to your inn and I'll tell you the whole tale.'

Soon you are back by the fireside, a goblet of mulled wine warming your hands as you recount your battle with the satyr. Fournil listens in amazement, drinking in the details. Now you have given him a story to tell his children!

Delete the codeword CHARON and turn to **97**

32

You are washed up on a stretch of grey sand. Raising your head wearily, you see in the north the dim silvery outline of the great plateau which marks the Wastes of Lagarto. Blind Fate has brought you to within sight of your goal! From here you must strike out inland until you reach the desolate fort known as Tarkesh Varn. That is the last western outpost of human settlement before the arid wasteland begins. There you can make your final preparations for the adventure.

Turn to **111**

As you press on towards the door leading to the kitchen-yard, you stumble into a pile of pans and bring them crashing to the floor. 'I told you to get out,' roars the head cook. 'Now look what you've done!'

'Hey . . .' realizes one of the servants, evidently more astute than his master. 'That's the barbarian they arrested last night!'

'Is it, by Tammuz, God of Plenty!' snarls the cook, snatching up a bloodied cleaver. 'Well, I don't think these barbarians are as tough as they make out . . .' He advances on you while the kitchen servants stand agog.

HEAD COOK   COMBAT 2   BODY 4

If you beat him, turn to **116**

You sprint to the end of the passageway, emerging into a vestibule with several doors leading off it. A servant is just coming out of the door directly ahead of you. You shoulder him aside, upsetting the tray he is carrying, and race past him into the prison kitchen. All around you, huge pots emit the steam and reek of boiled vegetables.

Hearing the commotion in your wake, the cook and two of his helpers take up cleavers and run to intercept you. You have no choice but to fight your way through them as you try to reach the exit.

HEAD COOK	COMBAT 2	BODY 4
SOUS CHEF	COMBAT 2	BODY 2
PASTRY CHEF	COMBAT 1	BODY 1

There is no room to flee past them, and the guards are close behind you, so this is a fight to the bitter end.

If you win, turn to **185**

35

You stand over the body of the satyr. It was a close-run thing, but in the end it was your foe, not you, who will sup with Queen Hel tonight.

You turn and peer into the darkness. Grinch and Grivois surprised you, scarpering like that. Not that you didn't expect treachery. You just didn't think they'd leave without the map.

The map—! You feel inside your jerkin, but it has gone. (Delete it from the list of items you're carrying.) You've been robbed, and you never felt a thing!

Hearing your bellow of rage, Grinch and Grivois peer back at the island and rock with laughter. The little beggars. You'd dearly like to make them pay. To think they had the temerity to trick a fearsome Norscan warrior like yourself! If only you could get your hands on their grubby necks, you'd show them the error of their ways . . .

Maybe you can. You're a strong swimmer. It would mean abandoning all your belongings, but you might be able to catch up with the punt.

If you try that, turn to **45**

If you have a bow and want to shoot at them, turn to **59**

36

The knight's manner becomes more friendly now. He tells you that his name is Sir Amanitas and he has lately come from the goblin market.

'What's that?' you ask, full of curiosity.

'A place where magic is bought and sold,' he says. 'I'll take you there if you wish to trade, but we must make haste if so. The market closes at moonset.'

If you agree to let Amanitas show you the market, he passes a cobweb handkerchief over your eyes and you can turn to **117**

If you tell him you'd rather get some sleep, he leaves you and disappears off into the trees – turn to **9**

37

Since breakfast is not yet over, the plates and cutlery have yet to be collected for washing. This means the scullery is almost deserted. There is only one maid here, who favours you with a bored look and a yawn before going back to her chores. The door beyond her is open, and the cool tang of pre-dawn air wafts in.

As you step past the maid, you notice a large cleaver resting beside the sink. At a pinch it would serve as a weapon. Take it if you wish, then turn to **129**

38

Your last blow cleaves the monster's head from its shoulders. It utters a dry voiceless moan and vanishes in a swirl of crimson light. You have given the lie to legend. Any foe can be killed – any threat overcome – if you meet it with a hero's heart.

You round on the snake. Now you'll have your revenge on the tyrant, by casting his soul down into the pits of hell.

You cannot overcome me, speaks the voice in your mind. But this time, instead of omnipotent assurance, it is laced with uneasiness.

'"No mortal man", was what you said,' you growl in reply. 'But, you Chaos-worm, I'm no mere mortal now. In overcoming all obstacles to get to you, I've stridden into myth. It's not a mortal you must face, but a hero!'

You raise your arm to strike, but at the same instant the serpent lashes out with a final spell. A vortex of roiling white fog opens under your feet, sucking you down into amorphous Chaos. Roll one dice.

If you get less than or equal to your MIND score, turn to **52**

If you roll more than your MIND score, turn to **92**

39

'What's this, then?' says the first rogue, the one with the eyepatch, pointing to a blob on the map.

The other peers at it, then rubs it away. 'That's me supper that I 'ad on the way over. *This* is the tomb, see? The sort-of pyramid with the settin' sun drawn next to it.'

'Blimey!' gasps the one-eyed fellow. 'It's 'alfway to the edge of the world!'

'Well,' counters his friend, nodding sagely, 'you'd 'ave to go as far as that an' back again for another treasure like this one's supposed to be.'

You've heard enough.

If you decide to muscle in on their game, turn to **25**
If you want to get another drink in first, turn to **53**

40

You set out from Runeport in the early morning, under a heavy sky that looks like a slab of shale. Clouds scud morosely ahead of a damp wind that promises rain later in the day. Cresting a grassy bluff, you stand surveying the wasteland that lies ahead.

To your right, gleaming like a tarnished silver plate, stretches the watery morass of the Marais Deperdu, the so-called 'Swamp of Lost Souls'. The mortal remains of many brave men lie deep in those insidious quagmires.

You turn your head to gaze directly west. A bleak vista of wuthering fells reaches off towards the distant blue outlines of the Massif des Geants, or Range of Giants, whose ragged ice-capped peaks scrape the very floor of heaven. Ogres dwell there; worse things wait beyond.

Neither route seems inviting. There is one other

way you might travel to the tomb, and that is to head directly south to the coast. There you could get a ship to take you west and drop you at one of the depot towns on the fringe of the great desert. Of course, passage on a ship costs money.

If you take the route through the swamps, turn to **106**

If you decide on the direct route, straight across the mountain range, turn to **67**

If you strike out southwards, towards the coast, turn to **76**

41

Before anyone can stop you, you have run to the side and thrown yourself overboard. The sea slams up past you, shock of the cold making you gasp. With limbs flailing, you strike up towards the gleam of steely light above. Your lungs are on fire, desperate for breath; your pulse thuds inside your skull. Then, just as you think you are not going it make it, your head breaks the surface. You draw in a deep breath and give a shout of lusty joy, grateful to be alive.

Ignoring the captain's shouts of protest, you swim off towards the shore. You are a good swimmer, but the chill is draining your strength. At each stroke you give a growl of effort, hauling your leaden limbs through the buffeting waves.

Roll one dice. If you score 1–5, turn to **13**

If you get a 6, turn to **3**

42

Magister Caenwulf's abode proves to be a bleak stone fort situated on a promontory extending out to sea. High waves crash against its ancient flanks, sending sprays of grey-flecked white foam up into the air.

You walk along the brine-slick promontory, oblivious of the wind that blasts icy drizzle into your face. Behind the clouds, the sun sinks unseen, leaving a gathering grey twilight as you reach up towards the rusted iron door-knocker.

After a while, a bolt is drawn back and a crabbed old man peers out into the dusk. 'Yes?' he says querulously. 'What is it you want?'

'I wish to see Magister Caenwulf,' you reply. 'I must journey to the ends of the earth, and I seek his help.'

The old man reluctantly admits you. Kindling a candelabra, he stands studying you in the draughty stone-flagged hall. 'You look like a barbarian,' he says at last.

'And so I am,' you retort, 'and yet I have more manners than you, for it's not I who am keeping a guest shivering here in the antechamber.'

'Guest, is it? The way I see it, you're more of an interloper. So tell me: why shouldn't I turn you into a hog and roast you over my fire – *hmm*?'

By the gods! *He* is Caenwulf! What will you say now:

'Try it and I'll carve you up as an appetizer!' Turn to **83**

'I need your aid against the forces of Chaos.' Turn to **56**

'I wish to buy magical potions and the like.' Turn to **69**

43

The prow of the barge nestles in amid the clumped reeds and touches solid ground. You leap ashore, landing with a damp squelch on boggy turf. Ahead of you looms a copse of closely grouped trees which fills the interior of the small island. You can see nothing in the thick shadows that lie there.

The scent of danger is in the air. You move forward warily, tensed for battle. The branches snag your clothing and mud sucks at your boots, but you press on.

Suddenly there is a figure ahead of you. His upper body is that of a muscular but overweight man, coarse hair covering his skin. But small horns sprout from his brow, and his legs are like those of a goat. So is his smell.

SATYR   COMBAT 3   BODY 3

The satyr's arms seem to be swelling larger and larger as you fight. Each round, add one point to his COMBAT score up to a maximum of 6.

If you are still fighting when his COMBAT score reaches 6, turn to **118**

If you beat him before then, turn to **150**

If you flee, make a note of the satyr's current COMBAT and BODY scores before turning to **159**

44

Roll one dice.

If you get less than or equal to your SPEED score, turn to **85**

If you roll more than your SPEED, turn to **58**

45

Discarding all your items, you wade out into the cold dark water. (Remember to reduce your COMBAT score by one point because you no longer have a weapon.) You swim swiftly but quietly, listening to the chortling voices of the two thieves getting nearer and nearer.

'Ah hah hah!' laughs Grinch. 'We certainly pulled a fast one on that daft geezer, didn't we?'

'That's fer sure,' replies Grivois. 'Shouldn't 'ave messed wiv us, should 'e?'

You seize the edge of the punt and pull yourself up, water running off you as you fix them with a malevolent grin. 'And you slimeballs should never have messed with me!' you snarl.

You must look like a spectre of vengeance rising out of the waters of the mere. The expression on the two miscreants' faces is one of pure terror.

Then you realize: it's not you they're looking at. It's something behind you.

If you whirl to face the monster, turn to **99**

If you throw yourself forward into the boat, turn to **126**

46

One of the fishermen takes you sailing along the coast until you are almost level with the eastern edge of the desert. 'Go north from here until you reach the citadel of Tarkesh Varn,' he says as he sets you ashore. 'It is the last habitation before the great desert begins. If a short stay there is not enough to deter you from your wild expedition, then I don't know what is!'

You laugh and shake his hand. 'I think I've come too far to back out now, my friend.'

He sighs sadly. 'I feared you'd say that. Well, may all the gods watch over you in that case.'

You wave until he has sailed back around the headland out of sight, then you start to make your way inland.

Turn to **111**

47

You squirm through the hole, emerging into a narrow passage from which two doors lead off. If you want to try either of the doors, will it be the first that you come to (turn to **186**) or the one at the end of the passage (turn to **115**)? If you decide to carry straight on to the end of the passage without delay, turn to **102**

48

You are hard pressed against such overwhelming odds. Much as you dislike running from a fight, in this case there is no choice. Managing to break free, you race across the vestibule to the passage. It takes you through the scullery into the courtyard.

Turn to **128**

49

With the satyr defeated, you help Fournil recover the punt pole and the two of you head back to the inn. Soon you are sitting by the fireside, a goblet of mulled wine warming your hands, and all the horror of your fearsome encounter with the satyr quickly fades.

'It was the very Devil himself,' is Fournil's opinion.

'No,' you say, 'just a creature of ancient times.'

But Fournil's mind is made up. He shakes his head stubbornly. 'You defeated the Devil . . .' he mutters in awe. Oh well, let him go on believing that. You have at least given him a story to tell his children!

Delete the codeword CHARON and turn to **97**

50

He hisses like an angry swan and flicks his sword from its scabbard. 'Then thirteen drops of blood will do just as well,' he says as he advances towards you.

ELF KNIGHT   COMBAT 4   BODY 6

    If you take an injury before you manage to wound him, turn to **64**

    If you score the first blow, then fight on and if you win turn to **77**

51

They unlimber their spears and spur their riding-lizards into a headlong charge.

FIRST NOMAD   COMBAT 2   BODY 2
SECOND NOMAD   COMBAT 2   BODY 2
THIRD NOMAD   COMBAT 2   BODY 2

No sense in fleeing – they would soon catch up with you on their lizards. If you win, you can take one of their spears if you want it and then continue across the desert: turn to **78**

52

With a titanic effort of will you resist the noxious enchantment that the serpent tried to weave around you. The floor under your feet is solid stone once more. Before the serpent has time for another spell, you lop its head off. It flies across the tomb chamber to land inside the circlet of the tyrant's crown, the golden light dimming forever in its eyes.

You help yourself to what you came for: a choice selection of gold and jewels from the treasure hoard. You leave the crown untouched. Then, leaving the tomb, you begin the weary march back to civilization. With the loot you've taken you can live like a king for months.

A barbarian king, that is. Not one of those civilized tyrants.

53

You go over to the bar, but the landlord merely stares at you scornfully and points to the tariff scrawled in chalk on the wall behind him. This reminds you that you have spent nearly all your money and have only a handful of coins left. Soon you must start looking for gainful employment. Not necessarily honest, just gainful.

If you go over and join the two furtive rogues, turn to **25**

If you leave the inn and go looking for adventure elsewhere, turn to **66**

54

On and on you journey, further west than any man has been before, apart from the devil Chungor Khan and the terrified courtiers who buried him here. The day stuns you with heat, the night with cold. The cold is worse, for that is when you do most of your travelling, shivering under the stars as you slog on for league after league. Unless you have a fur cloak you must lose two BODY points due to exposure.

At last, more than a month out from Tarkesh

Varn, you catch sight of marble ruins in the distance. Beyond them, the red flare of sunset illuminates the outlines of a pyramid. It is the tomb of Chungor Khan! Your wearying journey is over at last.

Stumbling on, you ascend a rock outcropping from where you are able to scout out the area. A wise precaution, as it turns out. In front of the tomb are a horde of manlike lizards, basking in the dying light of the sun. You count dozens of them, all flicking their tails sluggishly as the chill of oncoming night saps their vitality.

Something catches your eye and you go over to investigate. At first you thought it was a scrap of dry bark – though what tree could grow here in this arid wasteland? Then, lifting it, you discover that it is in fact a large lizard's skin. One of the lizards must have shed it, coming up to the rocks days ago to rub the old skin away like a snake. You can keep the discarded lizard skin if you like (remembering to note it on your Character Sheet if so).

If you want to go straight down to the tomb, turn to **91**

If you think it would be better to wait until dawn, turn to **105**

55

With a snarl, you draw your sword. 'I've had enough of this sheepdip,' you say. 'Now, order the helmsman to put in to shore or you'll be swabbing the deck with your own entrails.'

To your amazement, Athscar doesn't even try to reach for a sword. He gives a great bellow like a sea lion and comes at you with his bare hands, roaring for your blood!

The sailors just stand back and watch, not daring to get embroiled in such a vicious fight.

If you overcome Athscar, turn to **127**

If you flee, turn to **41**

56

'Very well,' says Caenwulf, 'I will give you aid in one form. You must choose what you need most for your venture: is it strength of arms, sorcery, or fore-knowledge of what lies ahead?'

If you choose strength, turn to **110**

If you choose sorcery, turn to **136**

If you choose foreknowledge, turn to **149**

57

Grinch and Grivois did not make the journey with you. You will probably never see them again. At least that thought cheers you up as you stand shivering in the icy teeth of the gale.

Delete the codeword PSALMS and then turn to **70**

58

The satyr gives vent to a loud booming laugh, smashing the tree stump down with all his great strength. Roll one dice. The number you roll is how many BODY points you must lose.

If you are still alive after that, turn to **98**

59

You send an arrow whistling off into the twilight. But the light is poor, and even for you it is a long shot. Roll a dice.

If you score 1 or 2, you have hit: turn to **151**
If you score 3 or more, you miss: turn to **160**

60

Lifting its sinuous tail clear of the waves, the serpent brings it crashing down on to your boat. The flimsy craft is instantly broken in two. You hear Ramasse give a shriek as he plunges over the side into the sea. There is no time to worry about him, though, since you have your own life to save. Plunging through the icy waters, you hastily discard everything which weighs you down. (Cross off every item you have except for the map.) Then you struggle towards the shore.

Luckily the sea serpent does not pursue you. Obviously it has swum back down to its submarine lair to lick its wounds. You swim to the beach safely and lie there gasping, recovering your strength.

You cannot return to the village. The shame is too great. Not only did you fail to kill the monster as promised, but you escaped with your life while poor Ramasse did not. Then another thought occurs to trouble you – what about the map?

Roll the dice.

If you score 1–4, the map is all right and you can continue on your way; turn to **121**

If you get 5 or 6, however, the ink has been obliterated by the salt water and the map is now illegible, bringing your adventure to an abrupt end.

61

Snatching a sword from the weapons rack, you stand in the doorway and let them come to you. That way they can only fight you one at a time. This means you fight the first guard *only* to start with, then go on to the second guard once you've defeated him, and so on. (Remember to note that you now have a sword, and can restore your COMBAT score to its normal value.)

FIRST GUARD	COMBAT 2	BODY 2
SECOND GUARD	COMBAT 2	BODY 2
THIRD GUARD	COMBAT 2	BODY 2
FOURTH GUARD	COMBAT 2	BODY 2

If you turn and flee, turn to **20**
If you fight and win, turn to **7**

62

The practice hall is little more than a barn where guards can practice and take exercise when the weather is too wet to use the courtyard. You search around, soon finding a weapons rack with a few old swords resting on it. You check them for balance and the quality of the blade, and have just chosen the best of a fairly poor selection when a voice rings out from the doorway behind you:

'You varlet! Stealing weapons, are you?'

You turn. A burly man is standing there in the chainmail tunic of a sergeant-at-arms. He has a fine sword in his hand, its tip resting lightly on the ground in front of him. His huge beard and bald head give him a fierce threatening look. You sense he will be no easy opponent.

'Better back off,' you say, hoping to avoid a fight. 'I can go out of here past you or through you – but whichever way, I'm going out.' As you step forward, however, he raises his sword and closes to do battle.

(Remember to note the sword you've acquired and to restore your COMBAT score to normal.)

If you want to try and get past him to escape, turn to **142**

If you fight on and win, turn to **179**

63

You search the bodies before throwing them into the lake. Their arsenal of murder implements quite appals you. The garottes, poisons and concealed knives are not at all the sort of weapon you associate with a decent warrior. You throw them into the water along with the corpses.

Of more interest is the map they stole (remember to write it back in among your items) and a money pouch which contains twenty silver pieces. No doubt stolen from some poor dupe. You can add this sum to your current cash, the total still only counting as one item of encumbrance.

Delete the codeword PSALMS. Settling down on a bed of rushes, you help yourself to Grinch's and Grivois's eel supper. Tonight *they're* on the menu, and eels will be doing the feasting. The thought cheers you as you doze off for the night. The next morning you wake before sunrise and set out on the path leading west.

Turn to **111**

64

He surprises you by suddenly lowering his sword. 'Enough,' he declares. 'Honour is satisfied. I have my thirteen drops of blood; I do not need your life.'

If you accept that the battle is over, turn to **36**

If you insist on mortal combat, return to **50** and this time fight until one of you is dead.

65

Unable to kill the soul-serpent, you nonetheless can easily ensnare it. It struggles, twisting its coils to and fro, but for all its efforts it remains trapped.

Free me, mortal, rages the voice inside your head. *Free me and I'll grant you the riches of my tomb.*

You laugh. 'They're mine already for the taking,' you reply, 'but I want only a few choice goods.' You help yourself to an armful of treasure and head towards the exit.

Why? whispers the trapped snake's telepathic voice. *You could have had it all . . .*

'And live like a king?' You give a snort of disgust. 'I'm a barbarian; that's not my way. I'll live well on this lot for a few months, and then when I'm broke I'll go seeking adventure again.'

Madness . . . replies the serpent.

You shrug. 'You call it that; I call it living. Goodbye, tyrant.'

And with that you leave, sealing the tomb behind you and so ensuring the tyrant's soul will be trapped there for all eternity.

66

Adventure and gold are hard to come by in Rune-port, but desperation and stark poverty make you persistent.

You encounter a rich merchant, but your efforts at freelance tax-collecting are not appreciated by the city militia, who seize you and throw you in the town gaol. This unsalubrious place is known locally as the Pits of Despair – a name regarded by many as a euphemism. You will languish there for a long time, enclosed by dank slimy walls and with only a faint crack of grey daylight penetrating the bars of your cell. 'Your adventuring days are at an end, my son,' was what the gaoler said as he turned the key in the door behind you. Never a truer word . . .

67

A biting wind beats down on your back as you slog across the moors, but it is nothing compared to the freezing chill that begins to close in as you rise up into the foothills. After a couple of days, hungry and chilled to the bone, you catch sight of the snow-capped peak of Mount Kringla. It looms like a stooping giant, head lost amid clouds black with their blizzard-load.

There is a pass through the mountains, reputedly inhabited by fey magical creatures who rejoice in bringing woe to mortal wayfarers. In contrast, the terrors of the mountain peak are purely physical but no less unwelcoming: treacherous snowdrifts, yawning crevasses, avalanches, the deadly blood-freezing cold . . .

You must choose: will you seek the pass (turn to **94**), or try scaling the peak and descending on the other side of the mountain (turn to **2**)?

68

While you are plunging out through the rolling surf they have plenty of time to swing the boat around broadside. Three of the grim oarsmen rise from their trestles and draw swords, ready to greet you with a welcome of cold steel. The bo'sun joins them after casting a harpoon which inflicts the loss of one BODY point. Deduct this point from your total and then fight:

BO'SUN	COMBAT 4	BODY 3
FIRST OARSMAN	COMBAT 3	BODY 2
SECOND OARSMAN	COMBAT 3	BODY 2
THIRD OARSMAN	COMBAT 3	BODY 2

If you win, turn to **95**
If you flee with your life, you can continue west along the coast on foot – turn to **147**

69

Caenwulf gives you a condescending look. 'Ah, so it's a goblin market you're after? Well, I'm not in the merchant business myself, but I'll steer you in the right direction. For a price. But here's the catch: you'll not know the price till you've already paid it.'
If you agree to pay his price, turn to **158**
If you refuse, you can leave and continue on your journey by turning to **147**

70

Engulfed in a blizzard that blots out all light, you stumble blindly and by sheer luck find a cave in which to shelter. You crouch there shivering, listening to the shriek of the wind as it blasts sharp fragments of ice against the mountain peak. It is like the howling of demons, that sound, and after a while it becomes more horrible even than the life-quenching cold. You press your hands to your ears and cower there, finally passing into a state of numbed oblivion that resembles sleep.

You awaken to find the cave mouth piled with snow. Digging yourself free, you find that the snow storm has blown over and now the air is clear as diamond. The sky above is a deep cloudless blue, rich and dark as the sea. The snow crunches crisply underfoot as you search for a way down the other side of the mountain.

Roll *two* dice as you make your climb down. If you score less than or equal to your SPEED, you reach the foothills without mishap. If you score higher than your SPEED, you slip and fall at one stage of the descent, losing 1–6 BODY points (roll a dice to discover how many).

Assuming you survive, turn to **143**

71

'I already have that,' he laughs, 'once you are dead!'

Uttering a great shout of victory, he brings the tree stump smashing down with all his strength. It slams into you with bone-crushing force, driving your body down into the soft earth. If you had been lying on solid rock you would have been killed outright. As it is, roll one dice: your score is the number of BODY points you lose.

If you survive this terrible injury, turn to **98**

72

The satyr tells you this is a wondrous ointment that will enable you to see things that are normally invisible to human eyesight. 'You need only daub a little on your eyes,' he declares. There is enough in the bottle for a single application, so use it wisely.

If you've now inspected all the items you have acquired, you can return to where you left the punt moored.

If you have the codeword PSALMS, turn to **16**

If you have the codeword CHARON, turn to **31**

Otherwise turn to **4**

73

It isn't easy at first, this walking on water. In fact it is like trying to cross a giant jelly. But soon you are stumbling towards where Grinch and Grivois have moored the punt for the night. They have made a small fire and are crouching beside it roasting an eel. You hear them cackling with vicious pleasure like a pair of old blackbirds.

'Wish we could've 'ung around to see the look on the brute's face,' says Grivois.

'Yeah, we fitted that barbarian up like a kipper, didn't we?' laughs Grinch. Or is it Grivois? You never could tell them apart. Won't matter much in a couple of minutes, though. Their own mothers won't be able to tell them apart then.

'Bloomin' 'eck!' they cry as you race up the shore towards them. Then they waste no more time on words, preferring to draw the wickedly sharp daggers that are their weapon of choice.

| GRINCH | COMBAT 4 | BODY 3 |
| GRIVOIS | COMBAT 4 | BODY 3 |

You can't afford to flee, since they have the map you need. This is a fight you *must* win.

If you do, turn to **63**

74

You swim back to the beach where the villagers are waiting. All witnessed your epic battle in the moonlight, and no doubt songs will be sung in the years to come about the tall barbarian who came out of the north and fought naked and weaponless against a terrible sea monster! You are on the way to becoming a true hero, and can add one point to one of your characteristics: either COMBAT, BODY, SPEED or MIND (your choice as to which).

However, your pleasure at victory soon curdles when you discover all your belongings are missing! 'Where are the things I left here?' you demand of the villagers.

'Your friends made off with them while you fought the serpent,' you are told.

You give a scream of red rage that makes the villagers quail. So, Grinch and Grivois have shown their true colours at last. They have made off with the map you need, but perhaps you can catch up with them yet. You know they must head for Tarkesh Varn, which is the last settlement on the fringes of the western desert. If you make good speed, you might even get there before them.

Nodding curtly to the villagers, you head sternly along the shoreline, trudging implacably on throughout the night. Delete the codeword PSALMS and substitute a new codeword: SNEYP. It means 'revenge' in the language of your homeland, and the revenge you'll take on those treacherous thieves will be bloody indeed.

Now turn to **121**

75

Looming out of the swirling veils of snow you see a crude stone hut. A candle glimmers behind a low, thick-framed window of green glass. In the last few steps you took towards the hut, the temperature seems to have plummeted drastically. Your teeth are chattering so badly now that you almost feel they might break, so you throw caution to the wind and stride right up to the door. It opens with a creak and you duck under the low lintel, finding yourself inside a musty little room lit by just the one candle. It is cold here, but at least you are out of the snow-storm.

'Is anyone home?'

No reply. You shrug and hunker down in one corner of the room, listening to the wind whistling under the eaves. Mindful of the warnings of folklore, you take the precaution of voicing a general disclaimer: 'If anyone hears me, let them know that I intend to take nothing from this hut. I shall shelter here, but I shall not search around for the larder nor look to see if there is firewood in the grate. The moment the blizzard has blown over, I'll leave, taking nothing with me but what I brought in.'

That seems fairly comprehensive. From the stories you've heard, magical creatures have less power to harm mortals who make a point of staying out of their debt.

Shutting your eyes, you slowly drift into a dream-troubled slumber.

Turn to **81**

Two days' journey brings you to the coast, and a dour little fishing village of closely clustered, low-eaved cottages. The locals stare at you as though you were a fiend from out of the grey mists of Niflheim.

You just get your boot into the door of the tavern in time to stop them bolting it. Apparently they are not fond of strangers in these parts.

'Begone, you're not wanted here,' murmurs the landlord, confirming your initial impression.

You force the tavern door open and stride in. 'I wish to hire a boat to take me west along the coast,' you announce, staring around you at the unsmiling faces. There is no reply. 'Come, now!' you say. 'Is the fishing so good that no-one has the time for a short excursion?'

The landlord scowls. 'Aye, there's the rub. For none of us now dares take his vessel out on the sea, for fear of the sea serpent which haunts these parts.'

'It was sent by an old wizard who bore us a grudge,' puts in an old fisherman.

'Now we are plagued night and day, and our very livelihood is threatenend,' declares another man.

'It will be the ruin of our village,' says the landlord, shaking his head sadly as he evicts a regular customer who can no longer pay for his drink.

If you agree to help these desperate people, turn to **108**

If you decide to follow the coast in search of another village, turn to **121**

If you return inland to try another route, will it be through the Titan Hills (turn to **67**) or up into the Swamp of Lost Souls (turn to **106**)?

If you wish you can take his sword. His armour would not fit you, since he was of too slender a build for any barbarian, but the shield could come in useful. While you have the shield, there is a chance that any blow struck at you will be deflected by it. Whenever you are hit, roll a dice: on a score of 1, the shield takes the blow and you are unhurt.

After noting any new acquisitions on your Character Sheet, turn to **9** to get some sleep.

At last the all-important question: do you have the map?

If you do, turn to **145**

If not (and you were warned early in the quest that it was vital to keep it) then turn to **137**

Tarkesh Varn is the last settlement before the start of the trackless desert wastes. Here is your last chance to buy the things you will need. Years of adventuring experience have taught you the value of good preparation. Although eager to set out on your expedition, you spend a day looking around the market. What items do you think might be useful?

a water flask .... costs 4 silver pieces
a pick-axe .... costs 4 silver pieces
a fur cloak .... costs 2 silver pieces
a lantern .... costs 1 silver piece
a sword .... costs 6 silver pieces
a crucifix .... costs 2 silver pieces

Remember to note down all your purchases and to cross off the money, then turn to **131**

80

You open your mouth to give the lusty battle roar of your people. But before you can even fill your lungs, there are two viciously sharp knives raised towards your throat.

The one-eared rogue shoves his face towards yours. He only comes as far as your chest, but that's near enough to smell his breath. You've passed open sewers that were more fragrant.

'We asked you nicely,' he says, 'now I'll say it in plain language: shove off, or we'll 'ave to carve yer liver out and pin it to yer face.'

You go to reach for your sword – remembering too late that it is in the weapon rack beside the door, where all good customers are supposed to deposit their implements of war. Obviously these two care nothing for tavern regulations, in addition to their other crimes.

If you tackle them bare-handed, turn to **107**

If you look around for something to use as an improvised weapon, turn to **120**

81

You awake to find cold white daylight streaming in through the dusty window. You get up and stretch, groaning at the stiffness of your cramped limbs. Your breath plumes in the chill air of the stone hut. The candle has guttered and gone out some time during the night, leaving a short stump of green wax. You now notice something that you overlooked last night: a haunch of salt beef hanging from a hook in the corner of the room. Your stomach gurgles longingly as you look at this. It would make a decent breakfast, perhaps washed down with mead from the clay jug on the floor beside it.

Decide if you are eating the beef. If you do and are wounded, you can restore two lost BODY points. Also, you might want to take the green candle; note it on your Character Sheet if so. Now it is time for you to be on your way.

Turn to **103**

82

You nock on an arrow and send it sailing into their midst. One of the oarsmen clutches his breast and you are satisfied to hear a bleak cry as he pitches into the water. The others ply the oars, swinging the boat around and heading back towards the *Heldrasir*.

However, the bo'sun is not prepared to let your attack go without reply. He hurls a harpoon with great strength, sending it soaring over the foaming brine to plunge into your shoulder. You scream in shock, staggering as hot blood gushes down your arm. Lose two BODY points.

You pull the harpoon free and stare through tears of dizzying pain at the departing boat. The bo'sun stands looking back at you. 'You seek Chungor Khan, who was our king in ancient times and will again be!' he cries. 'May you find him, barbarian – and his dread mistress too!'

A curious and not entirely encouraging statement. You ponder his words as you watch them climb back aboard their vessel and sail off.

Turn to **147**

'That,' says Caenwulf smiling, 'is fighting talk . . .'

He suddenly puts his fingers to his lips and gives a piercing whistle. In answer, a huge white wolf comes bounding down the stairs and launches itself at your throat. You must fight.

WEREWOLF   COMBAT 5   BODY 4

Note that it is difficult to hurt the werewolf with ordinary weapons: you will need a COMBAT roll of 1–2 on the dice to hurt it. (If you have a silver arrow, however, you can use this like a dagger. The silver arrow *will* affect the werewolf on a normal COMBAT roll, but it is broken in the fight and you must cross it off your Character Sheet afterwards.)

If you defeat the werewolf, turn to **96**

If you flee from here and continue on your journey, turn to **147**

84

You fetch your war-gear and throw open the door, demanding that Fournil punts you out to the island. Pulling a miserable face, he casts a reluctant glance past you into the rain-swept darkness. 'I beg of you, leave the devil where it is!' he bleats.

'Come, man, would you live out your days in cowardice?' you retort.

'In preference to meeting a grisly end at a monster's hands, yes,' he avers. 'Additionally, there is a good chance of contracting the flu if we go out in such weather.'

You snort derisively. 'Pah! Among my people, newborn babes are left to toddle nude in the snow so as to toughen them up. And you fear a little drizzle?'

Fournil shakes his head in feigned regret. 'Lacking experience in child-care, my parents merely left me swaddled in soft cotton throughout my formative years.' Nevertheless, he pulls a cloak over his shoulders and follows you lugubriously out into the rain. Climbing into the barge, he takes up his pole and starts to punt you out towards the island in the middle of the mere.

Note the codeword CHARON, then turn to **43**

85

You recover your wits just in time. As the stump comes hurtling down, you hurl yourself to one side. You hear it thud into the ground where you were lying just a split second ago. The impact splinters the dead wood and leaves a deep gouge in the earth.

Jumping to your feet, you round on the satyr. You are ready to continue the battle, but suddenly his massive arms begin to shrink until they are as thin as an old lady's. Apparently he over-exerted himself lifting the tree stump, and has now used up all his magical strength. Excellent. You close in for the kill.

Turn to **112**

86

According to the satyr, this ring can be used to immobilize an opponent by freezing them in time. He would have used it himself, but the band is too narrow to fit on his thick stumpy fingers – fortunately for you.

In any combat, you can use the ring to despatch *one* enemy without rolling the dice. If you are facing multiple foes, the others will be unaffected. Also, the ring only has enough sorcery left in it to work once, so think carefully before you use it.

If you now want to return to where you left the punt moored, turn to **16** if you have the codeword PSALMS

If you have the codeword CHARON, turn to **31**

Otherwise turn to **4**

87

The old man who is the cell's sole occupant thanks you for freeing him. He draws his tattered robe around him, managing to muster a shadow of the dignity he must have possessed before his long incarceration in this dreadful place.

'You go on without me,' he insists. 'I'm too slow to keep up with a young blood like you, and in any case I travel best alone. But I won't forget your kindness, and I want you to take this as a token of my gratitude.' He pulls a golden figurine of a mongoose out of the ragged folds of his robe and presses it into your hand.

'I can't accept this,' you protest, perhaps not too adamantly.

'It's nothing,' he says. 'A trinket only. Someday I'll repay you properly, though – be sure of that.'

You nod, wasting no time on farewells. Make a note of the mongoose figurine on your Character Sheet.

If you have not previously done so, you could now try the door to the guardroom – turn to **115**

If you do not want to go into the guardroom, or did so already, then turn to **102**

You stand in the middle of the cell with your back to the door, preparing yourself for battle. At last your patience is rewarded by the sound of footsteps and the key grating in the lock. 'Come on, you,' snarls a voice. 'Haven't got all day.'

You ignore him.

'Not in any hurry to check over the scaffold?' asks another guard nastily. 'But we had it built just for you!'

Seeing that you still remain immobile, one of the guards enters the cell. The scuff of his boots on the flagstones tells you his stance, left foot advanced towards you. You picture him in your mind's eye: sword arm held back, reaching for you with his left hand . . .

The moment you feel his grip on your shoulder, you reach up to seize the wrist, twisting the arm around as you turn. The other guard hears his companion cry out and rushes to join in. You must fight them both – and remember to reduce your COMBAT score by one point since you are unarmed.

FIRST GUARD	COMBAT 3	BODY 2
SECOND GUARD	COMBAT 4	BODY 2

There is no room to get past them to flee.

If you win, you can take one of their swords and then turn to **102**

The guards who attacked you have fallen, but there are more right behind. You turn and race across the vestibule, then along a short passage which brings you out into the courtyard of the fort.

Turn to **128**

90

You can use the genie once. He will appear beside you and fight as your companion, having COMBAT 5 and BODY 1. You must then roll at the start of each round to see if your opponent strikes at the genie (indicated by a roll of 1–3) or at you (a roll of 4–6). After the battle, the genie will vanish leaving you with an empty flask – which you can retain if you want.

Now turn back to **117** to finish your buying and selling.

91

Descending from the rocks, you confront the lizard-folk by the amber light of a dust-covered moon. Although lethargic in the chill of the night-time, several of the larger lizards come loping forward to fight you off. Behind them you see a huge dragon-like cockodrille waddling to the fray. There is a monster you're not keen to face!

You set your back against a narrow cleft in the rocks so that they can only come at you singly. This means that instead of every lizard getting to strike you every round (as would usually happen with multiple opponents) you only have to fight one at a time. Once the first is dead, go on and battle the second, then the third, and so on.

FIRST LIZARD	COMBAT 2	BODY 1
SECOND LIZARD	COMBAT 2	BODY 1

THIRD LIZARD	COMBAT 2	BODY 1
FOURTH LIZARD	COMBAT 2	BODY 1
COCKODRILLE	COMBAT 3	BODY 10
FIFTH LIZARD	COMBAT 2	BODY 1
SIXTH LIZARD	COMBAT 2	BODY 1
SEVENTH LIZARD	COMBAT 2	BODY 1

If you flee up into the rocks, turn to **105**
If you kill all your opponents (no cheating!) turn to **132**

92

The room drops away, leaving you suspended in a featureless white void. Chilling numbness seeps through your pores and stark Chaos floods over you, shattering your sanity. Is this death, or something far worse? You will never know the truth, for in Chaos's realm there *is* no truth but one. You know now that Chaos is like a vast storm-churned ocean and Law is just a tiny dyke of crumbling clay in the face of it. The final outcome could never be in doubt. Heroes like yourself can struggle against it, but they only stave off the inevitable. Eventually everything – adventure, life and the cosmos itself – must wind down into the hungry maw of Chaos . . .

93

You hold your tankard over the map and start to tilt it. 'I shouldn't leave that where beer might get spilled on it,' you say casually. 'Could ruin an old map like that.'

Mouths gaping in horror, they stare at the tankard and then at you. 'B-be careful!' cries the fellow who has an ear missing.

'Of course I'll be careful,' you say, squeezing into the seat beside them. Your shoulders are so broad that they are pushed right up against the wall.

'What do you want, then?' asks the one wearing the eyepatch, relaxing slightly as you set the tankard down.

'Another drink would do for starters,' you reply, tipping the tankard to show it is empty.

'There wasn't anything in it!' says the one-eared man with a gasp of outrage. 'You scurvy mongrel!'

'Now, now,' you say, pulling the map across the table for a closer look. 'That's no way to talk to your new partner, is it?'

Turn to **166**

94

Locating the pass, you struggle on as a blizzard casts high swirls of fine dry snow down from the mountain peak. Soon it is difficult to see a thing, and you are so cold that your limbs scarcely seem to be part of your own body, but still you force yourself to trudge onwards. The alternative is death, since the moment you ceased to walk you would start to freeze to death.

Then you see a flickering green light through the snow. Perhaps it betokens a huntsman's hut, where you could find shelter. On the other hand, you cannot help thinking of the eerie reputation of this gloomy place. The light could be a faerie lure, set to tempt you to your doom . . .

Choose now. Will you head for the light? If so, turn to **75**

If you ignore it and continue to press on through the blizzard-swept pass, turn to **21**

The remaining oarsmen stare at you like startled fish and leap overboard, making for the safety of their ship with powerful strokes. You gaze out over the waves, just able to make out the figure of the ship's captain where he stands dourly on the bridge. He raises his hand and the *Heldrasir* pulls further out to sea, quickly being swallowed up by the haze.

You are left in possession of the rowboat. Taking it along the coast, you soon come to a village where you are able to sell it for thirty silver pieces. There is no point in keeping it, so you accept the offer. Note down the money on your Character Sheet (it counts as a single item for encumbrance purposes).

If you want to make some purchases here in the village, turn to **148**

If you want to press on westwards, turn to **147**

Caenwulf stands watching the battle with arms folded. As you stand over the bloody carcass of the werewolf, he snaps his fingers and it transforms before your eyes, becoming a rug.

'Dry your feet,' says Caenwulf, 'then follow me through to the other room.'

You do as he says, wary in case of tricks. He is obviously a wizard of great power, and caution is needed. You are unsure how to proceed now.

The room at the back of the hall is a high-ceilinged parlour, given meagre warmth by a roaring fire. Caenwulf settles himself into one wooden chair and indicates for you to take the other.

If you do, turn to **56**

If you insist on switching chairs, turn to **123**

After a pleasant night's sleep, you are ready to continue on your way. Sitting in Fournil's punt, you watch your breath curdle in the chill morning air. The water slides by beneath you, smooth as a mirror. A light gauze of early mist shrouds the ominous island.

A strange cry startles you into reaching for your sword—

'The booming of a bittern,' says Fournil with a smile.

You relax. Soon you have reached the far shore of the mere. Thanking Fournil for his hospitality, you climb out of the punt.

'Where are you bound now?' he asks.

You consult the map. 'To Tarkesh Varn.'

'Then have a care,' he counsels. 'The folk there are odd, cranky in their ways. Strangers may easily fall afoul of their harsh laws.'

'I am fast becoming experienced in the snares and pitfalls of "civilized" life,' you reply with a grin. 'Farewell.'

Without waiting to see him punt away, you turn your face west and trudge off along a narrow wooded path leading up out of the marshes.

Turn to **111**

The pain is agonizing, but you cannot afford to let that distract you. Struggling to your feet, you prepare to sell your life dearly. That is all any Norscan warrior asks: the opportunity to die valiantly in battle.

The satyr steps forward, equally eager, but

suddenly his massive arms begin to shrink! Like balloons, the muscles rapidly contract until they are like two wizened twigs. Evidently he over-exerted himself uprooting the tree stump, and has now used up all his magical strength. Scenting a kill, you close in with teeth bared.

Turn to 112

99

You look round, expecting to see some ghastly lake-monster with many tendrils and a face full of fins and fangs.

There's nothing there. Of course.

Realizing too late that you've been suckered, you start to turn back. Before you can react, the punt pole lands squarely across the back of your head and you slump into the mere, unconscious.

Icy water closes over you. Fishes will nibble on your flesh tonight, while Grinch and Grivois will travel on into whatever adventure awaits at the tyrant's tomb.

For you, however, the adventure ends here.

100

You step through the door and immediately collide with a group of guards who have just finished breakfast. It takes them only a split second to realize you are an escaped prisoner. One tries grappling you as the others pull their swords from their scabbards. Within moments you are embroiled in a deadly struggle.

| FIRST GUARD | COMBAT 3 | BODY 2 |
| SECOND GUARD | COMBAT 3 | BODY 2 |

| THIRD GUARD | COMBAT 3 | BODY 2 |
| FOURTH GUARD | COMBAT 3 | BODY 2 |

If you flee, turn to **48**
If you win, turn to **89**

101

Hurriedly unrolling and spreading the Cloth of Marvels out on the ground, you draw it aside with a flourish to reveal a succulent feast laid out on golden plates. These are only faerie fruits – illusions conjured out of the dust and the air – but the nomads take them to be real. Climbing down off their strange steeds, they fall upon the food with great gusto, devouring huge handfuls of gritty sand under the impression that they're eating stuffed vine-leaves, pastries and spiced sweetmeats. Then, declaring their satisfaction with hearty belches, they stuff the golden plates into their saddlebags, clamber back on to the lizards and go riding off.

Within a day the gold plates will have turned back into pebbles, but by that time you will be far away from here. Note that the Cloth of Marvels is now a simple piece of silk, its magic used up. (If you keep it, change the entry on your Character Sheet to read 'piece of cloth'.)

You continue on your way. Turn to **78**

102

At the end of a winding corridor you come to a vestibule with two doors leading off it. There is also a narrow passage beside the door nearer to you. Just as you are deciding which route to take, one of the doors opens and the smells and sounds of cooking waft out.

You dodge back out of sight just in time. A servant emerges from the kitchen bearing several bowls of porridge on a tray. He crosses to the other door and goes through. As the door swings shut, you hear a voice saying, 'About time! Don't you know we've got to be on duty in a few minutes?'

Obviously the further door is the mess hall, and the nearer door must be the kitchen. The passage probably leads to the scullery or the kitchen-yard.

If you enter the mess, turn to **100**
If you take the door to the kitchen, turn to **170**
If you head along the scullery passage, turn to **37**

103

If you took *anything* while you were inside the hut –
    that is, either the beef or the candle (or both) –
    turn to **130**
If you left them untouched, turn to **143**

104

As he passes the guards, Grinch stumbles and blunders into one of them. 'Get off, you lousy beggar,' snarls the guard, jerking Grinch around by the front of his jerkin. You reach out to catch the guard's arm, but he has already given Grinch a rough shove that sends him flying.

You and Grivois rush over and help your companion to his feet. 'Are you 'urt?' asks Grivois. 'Didn't 'ave ter shove yer like that, did 'e?'

Grinch puts his hand to his head and sways groggily, steadying himself against you. 'I'll be all right in a mo',' he mumbles. 'Must've knocked me 'ead . . .'

'We'll find an inn,' you start to say, 'and you'll be fine after a night's—'

Suddenly you are startled by Grinch and Grivois both pointing at you with looks of outrage and yelling: 'Thief! Thief!'

You stare at them, a baffled half-smile on your face. 'Eh? What are you two on about?'

The gate guards come over and give you sharp looks. 'What's going on here?' demands their captain.

Before you can say a word, Grivois pipes up with an astonishing accusation: 'It's this barbarian, sir. 'E fell in wiv us on the road, an' now 'e's only gone an' stolen our dosh!'

The guard turns to you with a bored look. 'Give their money back, barbarian.'

'I stole nothing!' you protest, still confused. 'Grinch, Grivois – this has gone beyond a joke!'

''Ere, what's that e's got inside his jerkin?' says Grinch suddenly, pointing at you. 'Looks like a gold ring or sumfin'!'

One of the guards rips the front of your jerkin open and pulls out a gold ring that was indeed tucked inside it. 'Great gods!' he cries. 'This is my ring!'

The captain nods grimly and signals for his men to draw their swords. 'A pickpocket, eh?' he mutters.

'I swear to you, I never saw that ring before!' you tell him. 'Grinch must have stolen it, then planted it on me . . .'

The captain snorts and glances at Grinch and Grivois. 'You two, push off,' he says. 'We'll deal with the barbarian.'

As they go, the treacherous pair of rascals give you a saucy look and then you see something that makes you boil with rage. They have the map! Grinch must have filched it when he planted the stolen ring on you.

Cross the map off your list of items. Also, delete the codeword PSALMS and get a new codeword: SNEYP. Then you are led off by the guards towards the dungeons of the citadel.

Turn to **6**

105

You settle down for the night, managing to snatch a few hours' sleep despite your excitement. You know you will need it. In the predawn light you look down at the assembly of lizard-men. Crouched in the dust, they look so unmoving that they might be dead. But the sunrise sends shimmering heat up off the sand, galvanizing the lizards to life as it warms their cold unhuman blood.

You watch in awe as a great black reptile heaves itself out from the tomb entrance and waddles towards the lizards. By Thor, it is almost as big as a dragon! Peering about with blind milky eyes, it snuffles at each of the lizards in turn, identifying it by scent before sending it forth for the day's foraging.

Eventually all the lizards have gone. The giant cockodrille stretches itself out to bask in the sun. Being larger, it will take longer to draw full vigour from the sun's rays. This is the best chance you're going to get . . .

You descend from the rocks and cautiously approach the blind old cockodrille. Hearing you, it lifts its head and sniffs.

If you have a discarded lizard skin, it lets you pass and you can enter the tomb. (Turn to **132**)

If you do not have a lizard skin, the cockodrille detects your human odour and realizes you are

an interloper: you have a fight on your hands!
(Turn to 155)

106

Your boots squelch in the boggy heathland as you trudge into the north-west. Low clouds hang like city smog, allowing only a sickly grey daylight to reach the ground. Trees grow in stunted shapes here and there, skeletal brown forms stretching despondently up from the waterlogged mire. Along the bare branches sit hunched black crows, croaking evilly to one another across the marshes. You pass tangled clumps of reeds which remind you of lank corpse-hair. The cloying scent of mushrooms hangs in the air.

At last you arrive at the edge of a wide mere. To cross it you will need a punt. Fortunately there is an inn standing at the edge of the mere, and from the post outside there is tethered a long flat-bottomed boat.

As you approach the inn, the door opens and a young man comes bounding out to meet you. 'Greetings!' he cries, his cheerfulness incongruous in such a desolate spot. 'If you wish to cross Mithril Mere you have come to the right place.'

You nod. 'Apparently so, if you are the owner of that punt tethered there.' You dip your fingers into your money-pouch. 'How much will you charge for the passage?'

He smiles disingenuously and sniffs the air. 'Time enough to discuss that over a stoop of ale beside the hearth. Evening is coming on, and there is rain in the wind. It will be more comfortable to rest at my inn tonight and travel on tomorrow.'

You glower at him. 'And how much will that all cost?'

He shrugs. 'Oh, let's say seven silver pieces. Normally it would be more, but today I am in a merry mood and cannot be bothered to haggle.'

'If I gave you seven silvers you'd have good cause to be merry!' you retort.

If you have the codeword PSALMS, turn to **168**

Otherwise, you have the choice of paying the sum he asks (cross it off, then turn to **175**), trying to argue him down to a lower sum (turn to **14**), or stealing the punt (turn to **29**)

107

You might have just made the last mistake of your life. These two are small and spindly, but they are as nasty and cunning a pair of killers as you are ever likely to meet.

| GRINCH | COMBAT 4 | BODY 3 |
| GRIVOIS | COMBAT 4 | BODY 3 |

Remember to reduce your COMBAT score by one point because you are temporarily without a weapon.

If you win, turn to **133**

If you flee out of the tavern and go looking for easier pickings, turn to **66**

108

You soon learn that the sea serpent shows itself most often at moonrise, out among the sharp rocks off the coast.

If you decide to go to face the monster in a rowboat, turn to **153**

If you think it would be better to swim out, turn to
162

109

'The thing is,' says Grinch – assuming that Grinch *is* the one with the eyepatch – 'The thing is, we're goin' to 'ave to jump ship, see.'

'Yeah,' says Grivois, 'but we don't want to get our feet wet, do we? So we'd better wait till it's dark, then pinch the rowboat.'

Grinch rubs his stubbled chin. 'That's right, but who's goin' to row, if you don't mind me askin'?'

'What about the barbarian?' suggests Grivois after considering this for some time. He looks at you: ''Ow about it, chum? You're the strong one of the team. In fer a penny, in fer a pound, as they say.'

If you agree to man the oars, turn to **122**

If you refuse, turn to **135**

110

Caenwulf goes over to the wall and takes down a huge double-headed axe. It glistens in the candlelight as he hands it to you. 'This is the polearm known as Skullcleaver,' he says. 'It will stand you in good stead, I think, because it has a special power. On the first stroke in any battle, it always strikes true. I am told the first stroke is often the only one that counts. May it always prove so for you.'

Note that you have Skullcleaver. In any fight, you will always wound your foe on the first round without having to roll the dice. In subsequent rounds you will still have to roll equal to or under your COMBAT score, as usual.

Thanking Caenwulf, you return to the mainland

enraptured by your new acquisition and head on your way westwards.

Turn to **147**

111

You make good speed towards Tarkesh Varn, your thoughts full of the treasure you will wrest from the desert tomb. Then, as you are passing through a sparse grove of trees, you hear a strange sound. You stop and cup your ear, and then you hear it again: a faint reedy sound, like the far-off horns of Elfland . . .

It is getting close to dusk, and you should really be looking for a place to spend the night.

If you want to investigate the mysterious music, turn to **181**

If you prefer to press on towards your goal, turn to **188**

112

You lunge forward, but now that he is weakened the satyr has no stomach for further battle. 'Wait!' he says in a curiously high voice. 'Do not slay me, for it is without honour to butcher a helpless foe.'

You smile like a wolf and flick your sword-point towards his hairy throat. 'You didn't seem to think so a moment ago, when I was lying there stunned.'

His eyes flick down to the spot where the tree stump landed. It is half-embedded in the ground. It's a wonder that you aren't lying there under it. The thought makes your blood seethe, and you touch the blade to the satyr's bare skin.

'I'll give you my treasure!' he says hastily.

If you want his treasure, turn to **125**

If you don't trust him, turn to **138**

'You've got things a bit twisted,' you say, grabbing him by the scruff of the neck and shoving his hairy face into the hole where the treasure was buried.

You wait a few seconds, then release him. 'No, no!' he protests, spluttering as he spits out moss and wet soil. 'I spoke without thinking! Of course all the treasure is yours.'

You take the items you want. You can have the coffer too, if you like, though it is badly weathered and the lock is broken. Note these new acquisitions on your Character Sheet, along with the numbered sections that will tell you their special properties:

The shortsword (see **5** for details)
The jar of oil (see **72** for details)
The ruby ring (see **86** for details)

Once you have inspected all the items to find out what they do, you may as well go back to the punt. When you do that, turn to **16** if you have the codeword PSALMS or to **31** if you have the codeword CHARON.

If you have neither codeword, turn to **4**

114

You swim back to the shore to receive a hero's welcome. The whole village assembled to watch your epic battle in the moonlight. In the years to come, they will tell their grandchildren stories about the fearless barbarian who came out of the north to fight naked and unarmed against the terrible sea monster. You are beginning to carve out a legend for yourself, and can add one point to one of your characteristics:

either COMBAT, BODY, SPEED or MIND (your choice as to which).

As a reward the villagers present you with a purse containing twenty silver pieces. Note this on your Character Sheet (it counts as one item for encumbrance purposes).

The next day you ask again if someone will take you west along the coast in their boat, and this time you are inundated with offers. However, one old fellow called Fingus Redbise comes hobbling over and takes you by the sleeve. 'You don't want to go fleeting off like that,' he wheezes. 'You ought to go drop in on Caenwulf the Mage first. Mayhap he'd give you some help in your quest.'

'Foolishness!' snorts another villager. 'Don't listen to crazy old Fingus. He hasn't been right in the head since he got stranded on a sandbank and spent four days drinking saltwater.'

With more questioning you discover that Magister Caenwulf lives in a tower along the cliffs. Apparently he was a fearsome foe of Chaos in his younger days, and now that old age has made him infirm he sometimes gives aid to youthful adventurers. At least, that's the story. Your own experience with wizards is that they never do something for nothing. And you notice that the villagers seem pretty wary of this Caenwulf . . .

If you drop in on him anyway, turn to **42**

If you don't think you need his help, turn to **46**

115

The door opens and you stride boldly into a room where four guards sit playing knucklebones by the light of an oil lamp. They look up, surprised. It takes

them a moment to realize you are an escaped prisoner
– but only a moment. In that brief time you take in
your immediate suuroundings: the bunch of keys
hanging beside the door, and the weapons rack off to
your left. A number of swords have been left there,
along with one bow.

If you decide to run for it, you have time to snatch
one item first – this could be the keys, a sword
or the bow. Make a note of which you take and
turn to **20**

If you prefer to stand your ground and fight them,
turn to **61**

116

The other kitchen workers back off, horror draining
their faces white. Having seen you butcher the head
cook – the daily tyrant of their small world – they are
in no hurry to tackle you themselves.

You have time to snatch up the cook's cleaver, if
you need a weapon. Remember to note it on your
Character Sheet if you do. Then you barge past the
others and head for the door.

Turn to **128**

117

Now, to your amazement, you are able to see a path
of shining light wending between the trees. Following it, you soon come to a clearing filled with faerie
creatures of all shapes and sizes. Sweet music fills the
air and there is an enticing smell of spiced buns and
fragrant perfumes. Booths festooned with silk rib-
bons surround the clearing, and at each you see an
array of enchanted goods for sale. Stunned by the
many marvels on offer, you wander from one booth

to another, barely hearing the patter of the pointed-eared traders.

Among many other things, you discover the following bargains:

a Cloth of Marvels .... 7 silver pieces
a gold mongoose figurine .... 7 silver pieces
a lantern .... 5 silver pieces
a genie in a flask .... 12 silver pieces
a plague-curing potion .... 8 silver pieces
magical boots (add one point
              to SPEED) .... 5 silver pieces

(If you buy the genie, turn to **90** to find out more about it. The use of any other items will become obvious if and when they're needed.)

You might also want to sell items which you've acquired earlier in your adventure, and if you have any of the following then you can sell them at these prices:

Healing salve (per application) ..... 5 silver pieces
the axe Skullcleaver .... 40 silver pieces
the sword Propugnator .... 35 silver pieces
a magical ruby .... 24 silver pieces
a blue MIND amulet .... 21 silver pieces

When you have finished buying and selling, make the appropriate alterations on your Character Sheet and then you had better leave the goblin market and get some rest: turn to **9**

118

By now the satyr's arms are as thick as oak branches. He gives a last mighty buffet with his enlarged thews, and the force is such that you are knocked to the ground. As you lie stunned, the satyr turns and uproots a tree stump. Uttering an exultant roar, he hefts this above his head with superhuman strength. Mere seconds remain before he bashes your skull in with the tree stump. Will you:

Try to roll out of the way? Turn to **44**

Command him to put the stump down? Turn to **58**

Offer him a way off the island? Turn to **71**

119

Gold and jewels glitter in heaps all around. Ahead of you lies a marble catafalque, or grave slab, on which rests a skeleton the colour of old jade. Stepping forward, you hear a sound that sends a shiver of fear through your body. It is the sound of a serpent's hiss.

Rising from out of the skull's open jaw is a long green-black serpent that had been coiled inside the ribcage. It fixes its golden eyes on yours and a voice seems to whisper inside your brain: *At last – a living body for me to possess.*

This sounds bad. Evidently Chungor Khan's soul has lived on in the form of this serpent, and now he plans to use his sorcery to take control of you somehow. You move forward, arms raised to seize the swaying serpent before it can unleash its magic, but then the eerie voice comes again: *Foolish barbarian, you cannot kill me. No mortal man has the power to do me harm.*

If you have either a lobster pot or a piece of cloth, you can try using it to ensnare the serpent. Roll less than or equal to your SPEED on one dice to

do this. If you succeed, turn to **65**. If you fail,
turn to **24**

If you have a gold mongoose figurine and would
rather use that, turn to **192**

If you have none of these items, turn to **24**

120

The table is the only thing that comes to hand.
Bellowing like a mad bull, you wrench it up over
your head and use it to clobber the two astonished
thieves senseless. Then you pick up the map they
were poring over. It shows the region north and west
of Runeport: the tract of miasmal swampland known
as the Marais Deperdu, the hills of the Massif des
Geants – and, beyond, a great plain which gradually
declines into featureless wind-blown desert.

You are about to cast the map aside when you
notice something on the very western edge. It is a
symbol in the shape of an ancient ziggurat, of the sort
that great kings were buried under in times gone by.
Next to it is a large golden disk, no doubt indicating
treasure!

As you sit pondering the map, the two rogues start
to stir, giving weak groans.

If you leave the tavern while they are still
unconscious, turn to **156**

If you prefer to wait here until they come round,
turn to **146**

121

The next day, sauntering westward along the cliffs,
you spy a ship sailing quite close to shore. She has
black sails and a figurehead in the form of a huge
cackling crow's-head. Peering intently, you can just

make out the name painted on her bow: the *Heldrasir*.

A vessel of ominous aspect? Perhaps, but she is sailing the way you want to go.

If you hail the *Heldrasir*, turn to **134**

If you let her sail by, preferring to continue your journey on foot, turn to **147**

122

You wait until the dead of night and then creep over to the rowboat. It is suspended by ropes which allow it to be winched down to the sea. Grinch hisses a warning, and all three of you duck down as the officer on watch passes by on the other side of the deck.

'Right,' says Grivois, peeping out to check the officer has passed, 'we'll 'ave to look sharp before 'e comes round again. You lower the boat, barbarian, seein' as 'ow you're the strongest.'

'Better take off yer jacket,' says Grinch helpfully. 'It's goin' to be 'ard work rowin' all the way to shore.'

You peel off your jerkin and give it to Grinch to hold, then take hold of the pulley ropes and swing the rowboat out over the waves. Grivois keeps a lookout in case the officer on watch comes back. Straining with the exertion, you slowly lower the boat so as not to make too loud a splash.

Just as the boat reaches the waves, Grinch suddenly yells: 'All 'ands on deck, yer lazy tars!' and leaps overboard. He is swiftly joined by Grivois. As the officer on watch comes racing back, alerted by the noise, you go to jump after them. But you are pulled up short: someone has tied your belt to the main mast with a grappling hook!

You glare down to see Grinch and Grivois clambering into the boat and rowing away as quickly as they can. They look up at you with slightly sheepish grins. 'Sorry about nickin' yer jacket,' says Grinch, 'but we needed that map.'

Of course! The map was folded inside your jerkin. The cunning little—

You are seized from behind by several officers and whirled around to face the captain. 'You wanted to leave my ship; now you'll get your wish. By walking the plank.'

You are pushed out along the plank at spear-point until finally forced to jump. With your hands tied behind you there is no chance of swimming to shore. Green murk surrounds you, icy water fills your lungs, and you slowly drift down out of the world of the living . . .

123

He shrugs. 'All right.'

No sooner have you sat than wooden hands extrude from the arms of the chair to seize you in an unbreakable grip. You strain for all you are worth, but you cannot rise. 'You treacherous mage . . .' you snarl at him.

He puts on a wounded look. 'You call me treacherous? You should have been more trusting – the seat I offered you was perfectly safe.' To prove this he sits down in the other chair. 'Now, what shall I do with you?'

'Release me, if you don't want your scrawny neck snapped like a twig!'

Caenwulf stifles a yawn and stokes the fire. 'If only I had a log for every such threat I've heard, my poor old bones wouldn't be as cold as they are.'

'Wizard . . .' you growl in your most commanding

tone. 'Be warned: release me now, or face a Norscan's wrath!'

He seems to ponder this and for a moment you think you have succeeded in intimidating him. Then his seamed old face breaks into a sly grin. 'Wrath?' he mutters. 'That's it, then: I'll send you where you can discover what true wrath is . . . .'

He suddenly gets up and gives your chair a shove, tipping you over backwards. Unable to free your arms, you brace yourself for the impact with the floor, but it never comes. Instead you fall back into a swirling vortex of darkness. The room vanishes as though at the top of a deep shaft, down which you are plunging as if into icy water.

Suddenly you hit something solid. Snow! You have landed in a snow-drift. The chair releases its grip and you jump up, ready to avenge yourself on the wizard, but there is no sign of him or his manse. Or the sea, come to that. In fact, you are now on top of a high mountain: the dreaded Mount Kringla, highest peak of the Massif des Geants.

You can pick up the chair and take it with you if you want. It is heavy, counting as two items for encumbrance purposes.

If you had the codeword PSALMS on your Character Sheet, turn to **57**

Otherwise turn to **70**

124

Suddenly your opponent gives an animal snarl. Your blows have hurt it badly, and it wants no more. There is a reek of wet fur as it pushes past you, plunging into the black water of the mere. You wait, eager to continue the fight, but not even bubbles rise to the surface. Have you slain it? Somehow you think that's unlikely, but at least you managed to drive it off.

You return to your bed of reeds. If you lost at least one BODY point in the fight, note the codeword LUCTATION on your Character Sheet. (If you were not wounded, you do not acquire any codeword.)

You remain vigilant throughout the rest of the night, setting off at daybreak up the path that will take you out of the swamp.

Turn to **111**

125

He leads the way to a moss-covered bank of earth. Plunging his hands in, he extracts a small coffer from the soft soil. Once the coffer must have been quite fine, since you can still see glimmers of gold leaf here and there, and also tiny indentations where gems have been prised out.

'Some treasure,' you mutter. 'A rusty box.'

He lifts the lid. 'This is the treasure . . .'

You crane your neck to look inside. In the dwindling light you can just make out a gold-hilted shortsword, a jar of oil, and a ruby ring.

'You can take one item,' says the satyr. 'No more.'

If you wish to select an item, turn to **177**

If you contradict him, turn to **113**

126

You dive into a forward roll, expecting at any moment to hear the snap of some loathly creature's jaws just behind your neck. But there is nothing – no sound at all.

You look up. Grinch and Grivois at least have the

decency to look sheepish at the failure of their ploy. They glance at one another, shrug, and draw sharp slender knives. 'Look what's washed up,' says Grinch.

'Yeah,' says Grivois. 'All washed up.' You must fight them. Remember to reduce your COMBAT score by one point because you are temporarily without a weapon.

GRINCH	COMBAT 4	BODY 3
GRIVOIS	COMBAT 4	BODY 3

If you win, turn to **139**

127

Astounded by your victory over their tyrannical captain, the crew gather like a throng of ghosts around you. Then you realize that they are slowly fading away, like patterns of frost on a window warmed by the morning sun.

'You have saved us by lifting the curse,' says one of the sailors as he raises his translucent hands in front of his eyes. 'For centuries, that devil kept us as his lapdogs, doomed never to know rest, but now you've released us.'

They are all but gone now. Their last words are like the echo of a dream: 'Take our blessing, barbarian, for this great gift you've given us.'

You are alone on the ship, the sailors' souls having departed to the eternal rest they yearned for throughout the centuries. But their blessing remains, giving you the fortitude to face future perils: add two points to your MIND score.

Putting the ship in towards the coast, you take the

cutter ashore. In the north rises the silvery outline of the great plateau marking the Wastes of Lagarto. Good fortune has brought you to within sight of your goal. From here you must strike out inland until you reach the desolate citadel of Tarkesh Varn, the last outpost of human habitation before the arid wasteland begins. In Tarkesh Varn you can make your final preparations for the adventure.

Turn to **111**

128

You emerge into the open air. Grey pre-dawn twilight suffuses the sky. Seeing the main gate is open, you race towards it ignoring the sounds of pursuit. The two guards at the gate stir themselves, but you have run past before they realize what is happening.

Your headlong flight brings you to a narrow street. You must get away quickly, before your pursuers catch up with you.

If you race on along the street, turn to **171**

If you dart off down a side alley, turn to **140**

129

You emerge into the prison courtyard. A scaffold stands here with a noose strung from its crossbeam. No doubt it awaits your neck – not a fate for a Norscan warrior.

The sun has yet to rise, but the sky is now aglow with a limpid azure gleam, making it seem like a startlingly clear dome of glass. The stars are fading. Two guards are at the main gate, directly ahead of you, but they are lounging against the gatehouse and yawning. You guess they must be close to the end of their watch, and you may be able to slip by unchallenged.

You are halfway to the gate when you notice a long low building off to your right. There are a couple of stout wooden posts outside it, heavily scarred as if by sword-blows, and some wicker shields rest beside the open entrance. It must be the practice hall, where the guards hone their weapon skills. A good place to pick up a sword if you need one. On the other hand, can you spare the time to take a look?

If you enter the practice hall, turn to **62**

If you decide to make straight for the main gate, turn to **18**

130

You emerge from the hut into dazzling white sunlight. The sky is a wan bleak blue, clear and cloudless. Snow drifts are piled against the stone walls of the cottage and long prongs of ice dangle from the eaves. You shiver and pull your clothing tighter around you, stamping your feet for warmth. You do not notice the huge wedge of snow that has collected on the roof overnight. Suddenly it dislodges itself, smothering you as it falls to the ground in a miniature avalanche.

Spluttering, you pick yourself up and start to brush away the snow. Then you freeze – not from cold but from amazement, because a bunch of ice goblins are sitting on their haunches in the snow staring at you.

They are not like normal goblins, these spindly little fiends. They have faces like alabaster, their only colour the spots of blue on their cheeks. Their noses are shaped like icicles and they have eyebrows of hoar frost over tiny sparkling eyes. Each wears a coat of snowflake chainmail and has a glacier-hewn sword at his belt.

'Stealing from us,' says the leader in a thin fluting voice. 'Not a good idea.'

Smiles crack across the throng of white faces. 'Time to pay. Pay in blood,' they sing in a croaking, cackling chorus.

The leader takes a handful of snowflakes and blows them at you. Magically they become a flurry of thick white crystals, filled with a paralysing cold. Try to roll equal to or less than your MIND score on one dice.

If you succeed, turn to **154**
If you fail, turn to **163**

131

It is time to start your crossing of the desert. You go to the western gate of the city and gaze out across a shimmering plan wasteland of grey dust and scattered rocks. The sun streams down mercilessly, making the place chokingly hot by day. At night you have heard that temperatures drop to freezing. Small wonder that nothing lives in the barren wasteland of Lagarto.

If you have the codeword SNEYP, turn to **144**
If not, turn to **164**

132

The entrance of the tomb looms ahead, a block of darkness that engulfs you like a serpent's maw. As you stand in the entrance tunnel, you see a row of heavy stone jars lined along the wall. Opening one, you discover that it just contains sand – the same gritty grey sand you've been continually tipping out of your boots for the last month! If you want to take one of these stone jars, note that it is very heavy, counting as *two* items for encumbrance purposes. If you don't take one, you will have to smash the jars to get past.

You glance along the tunnel. The depths of the tomb are filled with pitch blackness. In order to proceed, you must have either a lantern or a candle. If you have, turn to **165**.

If you didn't bring a source of light with you then you have made a very serious oversight. You know that the slightest step inside the death-trapped tomb could spell disaster, taking you stumbling blindly into a bottomless pit or under a weighted block. Your adventure can go no further.

133

Rubbing your grazed knuckles, you go through the pockets of the two cut-throats. You find an astonishing array of murderous equipment including garottes, poison, hidden knives, blackjacks, and some implements that you are too innocent of such matters to even know the name of. You can take one of the knives if you wish, and there is also a money-pouch containing twenty silver pieces (the latter counting as one item for encumbrance purposes).

Then you pick up the map they were so interested in. It covers the region inland from here: the treacherous marshland called the Marais Deperdu, the forbidding Titan Hills – and, further west, a wide plain which gradually degenerates into lifeless wind-scoured desert.

You are about to throw the map away when

something catches your attention. There are some markings on the extreme western edge, virtually at the rim of the mortal world. There is a symbol depicting an ancient pyramid, of the kind used as tombs by monarchs in ancient times. Next to it is a shining yellow disk which no doubt indicates the presence of gold and jewels!

Turn to **156**

134

Your urgent waving attacts attention aboard the ship and a rowboat is dispatched. You hurry along the cliffs a short distance until you find a steep path which you can descend to the beach.

The rowboat is manned by silent rowers, hunched like gravediggers over their oars. The bo'sun stands in the prow, lank grey hair flapping in the salt breeze. When the boat is just a stone's throw from shore, he calls to you in a voice that is quiet but full of strength:

'So, if you would come aboard our vessel, wade out through the waves to us!'

If you insist that he brings the rowboat in closer to
    shore, turn to **157**

If you wade out to the rowboat as instructed, turn
    to **173**

If you attack them, turn to **12**

135

'Rowing won't be so hard between the two of you,' you say curtly.

They stare at one another in bafflement and shock. 'But what are you goin' to be up to while we're doin' our backs in over the oars?' complains Grinch.

You touch your sword hilt. 'I'll be making sure we aren't followed.'

The three of you wait until midnight before sneaking over to the rowboat. It is suspended by ropes so that it can be winched down to the sea. Grivois hisses a warning just in time for you all to dive out of sight. A moment later the officer on watch passes by on the other side of the deck.

'Right,' says Grinch, peeping out to check the officer has passed, 'we'll 'ave to look sharp before 'e comes round again. You lower the boat, barbarian, seein' as 'ow you're the strongest.'

You draw your sword. 'You both know the pecking order by now. Step to it.'

Grumbling sourly, they winch the boat down until it reaches the water. Then, as silent as spiders on a web, you lower yourselves down into the boat and scull rapidly away. After spending the night in a cove, you row along the coast until you come to a village where you are able to sell the boat for thirty silver pieces. Note down the money on your Character Sheet (it counts as a single item for encumbrance purposes).

If you want to make some purchases here in the village, turn to **148**

If you want to press on westwards, turn to **147**

136

He raises his eyebrows. 'Sorcery, is it? And here, I always thought you barbarians were so mistrustful of sorcery. Still . . .' He cups his hands and blows into them, then opens them to reveal a sparkling amulet comprising a smooth blue stone set into a gold surround.

'What's this do?' you ask, putting the amulet around your neck.

'It defends against magic. That's what you wanted, isn't it?'

You can increase your MIND score by two points as long as you retain the amulet. (Note this on your Character Sheet as 'Blue Amulet: +2 to MIND'.) Thanking Caenwulf, you return to the mainland and press on into the west.

Turn to **147**

137

Days pass but you see no sign of life. The sun beats down, blistering your skin and half-blinding you with its relentless glare. As dusk approaches, fierce winds thunder across the plains bringing a terrible sandstorm. You seek shelter, huddling behind a boulder, but even when the wind dies down you are not safe, for now the air grows colder and colder until you are shivering uncontrollably.

Weather-beaten, sun-burned, frozen and weak with thirst, you slump to the ground and wait for the grip of oblivion to grant you mercy. Your bleached bones will crumble here, becoming one with the grey desert sand.

138

Half-hearted and bone-weary, the satyr puts up the best fight he can against your ferocious onslaught.

SATYR   COMBAT I   BODY I

When you kill him, turn to **150**

139

You search the bodies before rolling them out of the punt into the water. Along with a quite appalling selection of insidious murder weapons, which you discard, you find the map they filched from you and a money-pouch containing twenty silver pieces. You can add this sum to your current cash (the total still only counts as one item of encumbrance).

Delete the codeword PSALMS. Taking up the punt pole, you whistle merrily to yourself at a job well done as you return to the island to retrieve the items you discarded earlier. Then, as the moon sinks in the west, you steadily cross to the far shore.

Turn to **4**

140

A mistake. You turn into a blind alley and, before you can retrace your steps, guards from the fort come pouring along the alley after you. Escape is impossible. You are swiftly surrounded. Despite a valiant struggle, the odds are overwhelming and you are swiftly recaptured, then taken back to your cell, where a constant vigil is kept until it is time for your execution.

You are led out to the scaffold, and the hangman slips the noose around your neck. You take a breath, see the grisly excitement on the faces of the guards, hear a panel drop away. There is a moment of weightlessness, followed by a blaze of light . . . and then silence, for ever.

141

You conceal yourself under a pile of rags and lice-ridden blankets in the far corner of the cell. At a casual glance the cell looks empty – and when the guards arrive that is exactly what they think. They are so startled by the sight of the gap in the wall that they do not even glance at your hiding-place.

After a moment of slack-jawed astonishment, one of them yells, 'Escaped prisoner! Sound the alarm!' They run off to fetch their comrades, leaving the cell door open. You follow at a circumspect distance, slinking off into the shadows of a side passage as they come racing back with reinforcements.

Now, with most of the prison's available guards searching for you through an escape hole that you never used, you are able to saunter out into the open unobserved.

Turn to 129

142

You charge at the sergeant, sword raised high as if you intend to chop down at his head. Your real intention, though, is to distract him while you run past and through the open doorway.

Roll one dice.

If you score less than or equal to your SPEED, turn to 187

If you score greater than your SPEED, turn to 180

143

Trudging through the deep snow-drifts, you make your way down out of the high pass. Soon there is green grass underfoot and a warm sun on your back, and all memory of the ghastly freezing mountains disappears like last night's dreams.

Turn to 111

Without the map, you will have to make the best speed you can and hope to catch up with the villainous Grinch and Grivois. You are not sure exactly which direction they would have gone – only that the tomb lies vaguely west of here. You have nothing to rely on but guesswork.

If you head directly westwards, turn to **23**

If you head west by south-west, turn to **137**

What about a flask?

If you have one, you can use it to gather water at the few meagre oases you pass every few days, and you will be able to cross the desert without dying of thirst: turn to **54**

If you do not have a flask, things look grim: turn to **137**

They sit up, nursing the contusions caused when you hit them with the table. The one with the eye-patch gives you a black look.

'Better put a raw steak on that,' you say, 'or you won't be able to see anything at all by tomorrow morning.'

He snarls, but both have learned to be more respectful of you now. Also, you have their map. They get warily up off the floor and sit down opposite you. 'What's your game, barbarian?' says the other rogue, the one lacking an ear.

'Same as yours, chum,' you reply, folding the map and stuffing it inside your jerkin. 'I'm going looking for buried treasure. Me and my two partners, that is . . .' You smile at them, letting them know who's boss, and push your empty tankard across the table. 'Mine's a pint, by the way.'

Turn to **166**

147

Two more days' walking brings you to a point level with the eastern edge of the Wastes of Lagarto. You look inland towards the high arid plateau that marks out that vast cold desert. From here you must strike out north towards the lonely citadel of Tarkesh Varn, the last human settlement before the desert begins. Once there, you can make your final preparations for the adventure.

Turn to **111**

148

In such a small village there are not many items to interest the dedicated adventurer. However, you do manage to find the following:

a water flask	costs 1 silver piece
a lantern	costs 3 silver pieces
a net	costs 9 silver pieces
a fishing rod	costs 6 silver pieces
a lobster pot	costs 4 silver pieces

Make any purchases you want and cross off the money.

If you are then ready to continue on your way, turn to **147**

If you try asking if there is anyone from whom you could buy some more interesting items, turn to **174**

'The tyrant Chungor Khan made himself unkillable,' Caenwulf tells you. 'So how did he die? That is a matter of dispute, like all legends. Some say he is not dead, but resides in his tomb waiting for a new shell of flesh in which to roam the world. That mad tyrant can put on bodies as other men put on a new suit of clothes.'

'How do I defeat him?' you ask.

'Not easily. If you can find a Cloth of Marvels, it might serve you well in more ways than one. Don't make the mistake of discarding something just because it seems useless. And don't overlook the obvious. You're crossing a desert to plunder a stone-walled tomb: you need bare essentials more than you need fancy magic! You'd do well to consider your purchases in Tarkesh Varn, and be sure you have some money left to spend when you get there.'

You nod, trying to look as if you're taking all this in. 'And how do I get to Tarkesh Varn?'

Caenwulf snorts. 'Walk! It's north-west of here, on the edge of the Lagarto Desert. Did you know that "largarto" means "lizard"? I thought not – you barbarians are so ignorant!'

'We're famous for it,' you say with a smile. 'Was there anything else?'

'There's one thing,' he says. 'When you get to the shore, pick up a pebble with a hole in the middle. It's what folk call an "elf-bored" stone. Worth having, I can assure you, even if you have to drop something else to carry it.'

Thanking him, you make your way back to the mainland. On the beach, you scour around in the moonlight for a while until you find one of the pebbles he described. Note this on your Character Sheet, then turn to **147**

150

Satyrs are very long-lived creatures. In fact, if the ancient myths are to be believed, they are immortal. That's assuming somebody doesn't come along and kill them. Such hoary beings have many opportunities to gather treasure throughout the centuries . . .

Greedily you make a quick search of the island, but you cannot find so much as a single gold trinket. You utter a curse, realizing that the light is going and it might not be safe to linger overnight. Since the satyr dwelt here, other supernatural entities might also make their lairs on the island. You return to where you left the punt moored.

If you have the codeword PSALMS, turn to **16**
If you have the codeword CHARON, turn to **31**
Otherwise turn to **4**

151

You are satisfied by the sound of a bleak cry as one of them drops into the bottom of the boat, impaled by your well-aimed arrow. They are too far away for you to tell which of them you hit.

'Aye, come on back and I'll make pincushions of the pair of you!' you shout, shaking your fist. But the other thief is in no hurry to risk your wrath, and instead punts as fast as he can to the shore of the mere.

The distance is too great for another shot. You were lucky with the first. Settling down for the night, you find that seething rage makes sleep hard to come by. The next day you awaken tired and in bad sorts, uttering many curses as you go about fashioning a makeshift raft. This raft is not sturdy enough to hold you, but it isn't meant to. You only need it to load your belongings on to so that you can tug them behind you as you swim over to the shore.

The water is cold, but it does nothing to quench your red rage. As you dry yourself off, you make a blood-vow: Grinch and Grivois will die for their perfidy! Delete the codeword PSALMS and get a new codeword: SNEYP. Then turn to **111**

152

You bide your time until, at last, you hear the footsteps of the gaoler bringing your supper. Hastily you spread the Cloth of Marvels, whisking it aside to reveal a transitory image. The gaoler slides open the panel in the door and raises a cup of gruel to the bars. Then you hear him give a gasp of surprise, for he has seen what your magic has wrought.

In reality you know the cell has not changed – it is still clammy, dingy, infested with vermin. But, by dint of the Cloth's magic, the gaoler beholds a different sight: a vision of gold stacked to the ceiling, of glittering jewels and caskets full of rubies like giant drops of blood.

Excited fingers fumble with the key. The door is flung open and the gaoler rushes inside, laughing wildly, to hurl himself at the pile of filthy rushes that served as your bed. The enchantment causes him to see it as extravagant jewellery, and he holds each rush up in the torchlight and mutters, 'Rich . . . ! I'm rich . . .' His rheumy eyes light up with greed, his tongue slavers across thin lips.

The weak-minded dolt. You put paid to him with a

swift clout to the back of the neck, then hurry from the cell. You can take his keys if you wish. Remember to cross off the Cloth of Marvels, as you have now used its magic. (However, if you want to keep it anyway you can now note it on your Character Sheet as 'piece of cloth'.)

Turn to **102**

153

No-one is in any hurry to accompany you, but finally an old man named Ramasse agrees to row the boat. 'You will need both hands free to battle the monster,' he says.

You nod, admiring his bravery. Perhaps you would prefer to go alone to fight the sea serpent, but Ramasse is right. At least he is an old man, with most of his life behind him.

That night the two of you take a boat out among the rocks and wait. The sea is calm – a mirror of indigo glass. At last the moon rises, creamy light spreading in gleaming veins across the water.

Less than a minute passes. Barely has the moon's disk risen clear of the eastern horizon when a vast waterspout shoots up, heralding the arrival of the monster. Then its head lifts out of the sea, and for a moment you feel a sensation which any other warrior would know as fear. But to you it is only an urgent pumping of the heart, a quickening of the blood. Fear to you is the fuel for ferocity. Uttering a blood-curdling roar, you swing your sword against the serpent's flanks.

SEA SERPENT   COMBAT 3   BODY 5

If it is still alive after five rounds, turn to **60**
If you kill it before then, turn to **114**

154

Chittering evilly, the ice goblins whip out their slim glistening blades and close in on you.

FIRST ICE GOBLIN	COMBAT 3	BODY 1
SECOND ICE GOBLIN	COMBAT 3	BODY 1
THIRD ICE GOBLIN	COMBAT 3	BODY 1
FOURTH ICE GOBLIN	COMBAT 3	BODY 1
FIFTH ICE GOBLIN	COMBAT 3	BODY 1
SIXTH ICE GOBLIN	COMBAT 3	BODY 1
SEVENTH ICE GOBLIN	COMBAT 3	BODY 1

If you flee, turn to **172**
If you fight on and kill them, you can descend out
    of the mountains by turning to **143**

155

The cockodrille snaps its long jaws and rears up, tail swinging like a battering ram. This will be a battle-royal.

COCKODRILLE   COMBAT 4   BODY 10

If you win, you can get past it and enter the tomb:
    turn to **132**

156

Remember to record the map on your Character
    Sheet. *Guard it with your life, since you cannot*
    complete the quest without it.
You have a long journey ahead of you. If you have

some money and wish to buy supplies, turn to
26

If you have no money, or prefer to conserve it in
case of later need, turn to **40**

157

'That I cannot do,' he answers, 'for my captain has
sworn none of us will set foot on land until the return
of his liege lord. This lord, whom my master long
served as admiral of his fleet, was a great conqueror
in times gone by. The plotting of spiteful courtiers
laid him low, cast him into exile in that bleakest of
lands that lies beyond the setting sun, but it is
prophesied he will come back. Until that day we stay
at sea, shunning solid ground.'

If you wade out to the rowboat, turn to **173**

If you attack, turn to **12**

If you decide to continue west on foot after all,
turn to **147**

158

Caenwulf leans over and embraces you. His spindly
arms barely encircle your shoulders, but then you
feel a queer sensation, and it seems as though your
frame diminishes slightly while his grip grows
firmer. As he stands back, you are sure that some
sort of change has come over him. Yes – he is
younger! While you . . .

'You've guessed,' he says almost apologetically.
'I've taken some of your youth. Oh, not much, just a
year or two. You'll hardly miss them, but they mean
a lot to one as old as me.'

You glare at him under beetling brows. 'Now your
side of the bargain,' you say curtly.

He smiles. 'Yes, the magic market. You'll find it if you do as I say. When you leave, go to the beach and find a pebble with a hole through the middle. An "elf-bored stone" is what we sorcerers call such things. Carry it with you.' He starts to turn away.

'Is that all?' you call after him.

He half turns. 'Yes – Oh . . . no, there's one other thing. Close the door on your way out.'

Scowling, you make your way back to the mainland. On the way you realize that you are not as fast and agile as you were before. Lose one SPEED point. Having reached the shore, you scour around by moonlight for a while until you find one of the pebbles he described. Note this on your Character Sheet if you decide it's worth keeping, then turn to **147**

159

You crash back through the thickets with the lusty laughter of the satyr ringing in your ears.

If you have the codeword PSALMS, turn to **176**

If you have the codeword CHARON, turn to **15**

If you have neither, turn to **30**

160

The arrow falls short. Far off in the gloom, Grinch and Grivois do not even notice that you've shot at them. You bite your lip angrily and start to turn away—

Suddenly a flash of glimmering whiteness catches your eye. To your astonishment, a slim pale arm comes snaking up out of the black water to catch your arrow. A ripple of luminous bubbles forms a track towards the island, and you can only stand dumbfounded as a woman clad in sheer white samite rises out of the mere in front of you.

'This is yours.' She holds out the arrow.

You take it. You cannot find any words.

Her laughter is like the tinkling of tiny glass bells. 'I am the Maiden of the Mere. Beneath the water lies my palace of lunar marble, with its decorations of sky-silver studded with star jewels. Join me there tonight. Be my guest.' She offers you her hand.

If you refuse her invitation, turn to **169**

If you accept, turn to **178**

If you explain that you are on a quest, turn to **184**

161

Taking up the bow, one of the guards nocks on an arrow and shoots at your retreating back. You cry out as searing pain rips through your shoulder. Lose two BODY points.

If you survive, you put on a burst of speed, darting around a bend in the passage before he can shoot again.

Turn to **34**

162

You realize that venturing out in a boat is too dangerous. The serpent might easily capsize it, and then you would be really sunk, to coin a phrase.

Instead you wait until dusk and then go down to the foreshore. The villagers watch amazed as you strip down to a loin-cloth, placing all your belongings in a neat pile on the sand. They would only weigh you down in the struggle to come. (Cross off all the items on your Character Sheet. You will be able to retrieve them later if you survive the battle.)

Plunging out into the water, you swim over to the rocks and wait for moonrise to tempt the sea serpent from its lair. You are not kept waiting long. No sooner has the moon appeared in the eastern sky than a great dark worm-like shape comes poking up from the waves. Its jaw agape, the monster rushes to meet you . . .

SEA SERPENT   COMBAT 3   BODY 5

Remember to reduce your COMBAT score by one point because you currently do not have a weapon.

If you defeat it, turn to **74** if you have the codeword PSALMS

If you do not have that codeword, turn to **114** instead

163

You are encased in a block of unbreakable ice. As the cold turns your blood sluggish, the darkness of death descends around you. Your last sight is the grinning faces of the goblins, distorted by the icy sheath, as they gather to gloat at your frigid fate.

164

Long hours tumble into days, and still you slog relentlessly on into the west. You soon discover that it is best to travel by night, when exertion keeps you warm despite the bitter chill. In the scorching heat of the day, you huddle in the shade of rocks and snatch a few hours of swooning sleep.

Do you have the codeword LUCTATION?

If you do, turn to **189**

If not, turn to **182**

You continue down deep into the warren of tunnels beneath the pyramid. At last the flickering light picks out a massive stone door decorated with intricate carvings. You peer at these in the gloom. The writing means nothing to you, but you can understand that the pictures show the funeral procession of a mighty king. You have reached the tomb chamber.

Something catches your eyes and you glance up to see two metal pans hanging from chains in the ceiling. They remind you of a set of scales – but what would you want to weigh?

If you have a stone jar full of sand and want to use it now, turn to **183**

If you think a pick-axe would be more use (assuming you have one) then turn to **10**

If you have neither of these items then you have reached a dead end. You slump to the floor, now noticing the littered bones of other failed adventurers who got no further than this. Exhausted and thirsty, you can only sit and futilely dream of the treasure that lies on the other side of the door – so near, but forever out of reach . . .

Your new-found cronies are called Grinch and Grivois. At least, those are the names they give you. After an initial reluctance in coming to terms with the new situation (you have to cuff Grinch for trying to slip poison in your tankard), they begin to accept you as their partner. Then you drop the bombshell:

'*Boss!*' they cry together. 'Why should you be the boss?'

'Because I've got the map and I'm keeping it,' you reply reasonably. 'Now, tell me the whole story.'

They grumble, but finally seem to accept this further turn of events. 'Awright,' says Grinch, 'it's like this. 'Undreds of years ago there was a geezer in charge of the whole of Norsca, and probably a lot more as well. Evil as an old crow, he was, and more money that you could stuff down a dragon's gullet. When 'e died, they buried 'im with all 'is loot, right on the very edge of the world—'

'Or at least the map,' puts in Grivois.

'Yeah. Anyway, 'e 'ad this pact with a snake goddess, see, so no-one dared take even so much as one gold coin away before they sealed the tomb. Too afraid of the goddess's curse.'

'And you two?' you ask. 'Why aren't you afraid of the goddess's curse?'

'We paid an old scribe to check out the legend,' supplies Grivois. 'We wanted to know the exact wording of the curse. Apparently, anyone who plunders the tomb will suffer "eternal damnation".' He looks at you, waiting for the light to dawn.

It must be too late in the evening. You have to ask, 'And . . . ?'

'Well, what do you fink?' he says, spreading his hands. 'In a profession like ours, eternal damnation's sort of an occupational hazard, as yer might say. Reckon we can forget about collectin' wings and an 'arp when we turn up our toes. Might as well get a bit o' cash to cheer us up in our declining years, though.'

If you still want to accompany them to the tomb, turn to **11**

If you are deterred by this talk of a curse, you

might prefer looking for easier pickings somewhere in the backstreets of Runeport; turn to **66**

167

The *Heldrasir* is far from land when you decide to
make your bid for freedom. You gaze down at the
roiling icy waters with a feeling of trepidation:
although a strong swimmer, you are not sure you can
make it to dry land. In the end, though, you decide
there is no choice. You have already realized that the
Heldrasir is a cursed ship, doomed to roam the seas
endlessly while her insane captain still pledges his
loyalty to a dead tyrant. You have no desire to share
that doom.

You make what few preparations you can, packing
your belongings in tightly wound pieces of oilskin
and coating your body with lard as protection from
the cold. Then, in the dead of night, you go to the
rail and jump overboard.

You swim on and on until fatigue racks your
limbs. Chilled from outside, burning with effort
inside, you feel as though you have been caught
between Surt and Ymir – the Giant of Fire and the
Giant of Ice in Norscan mythology. Salt waves sting
your eyes. Each breath is torn from the air hurriedly,
a great gulp, before the sea crashes down over your
brow again.

Roll one dice. If you score 1–3, turn to **32**

If you get 4 or more, turn to **3**

168

''Ang on a minute, matey boy,' says Grivois,
stepping forward to put an arm around the young
man's shoulders.

'Can we 'ave a private word wiv you?' adds Grinch, taking his arm and leading him towards the inn. 'In yer office, like?'

The young man smiles uncertainly as they disappear inside with him. You wait less than half a minute, then Grinch and Grivois emerge alone from the inn.

'Well, that's that sorted,' announces Grivois. ''E's givin' us the punt.'

You stare at him suspiciously. '*Giving* it? Just like that?'

Grinch returns your scrutiny with a sheepish grin. 'Yeah. Wot a generous bloke, eh? Shows there's still a bit of decency left in the world, dunnit.'

'Not where you two are concerned,' you mutter darkly. But nonetheless you join them in the punt and head out across the mere.

Late afternoon sunlight trickles half-heartedly across the water, creating a glint of pallid whiteness. As the punt slides on across the mere, you catch sight of a small island in the middle.

If you stop to investigate, turn to **43**

If you prefer to press on, turn to **4**

169

She smiles, but it is not a look of pure goodwill. 'Too many refuse me nowadays,' she murmurs. 'Too many are like you, preferring your grimy war-gear and your Chaos-battles over the sweet delights of true enchantment. Well then, so be it: if you will not enter my world now, nor will you ever again.'

She stamps her foot lightly in the rushes and turns, slipping off into the water like a fish. The water closes over her head and she is gone.

You ponder her parting words. They had an ominous ring to them. Rather like a curse. For a moment your skin crawled, but that might simply have been from superstitious dread. Even so, feeling it to be unwise to part from the strange maiden on such a sour note, you think it's best to try calling her back. You step forward into the water . . .

Or rather you don't. You step *on to* the water!

Gazing down at your feet, you can hardly believe it. Instead of sinking into the mere, you are standing on the surface. It feels like standing on a huge sheet of rubber. That was what the maiden meant, then. She has cursed you so that you can never enter water again.

You laugh delightedly. She meant this as a curse, but you see it as a blessing. Now you can walk across the mere in pursuit of Grinch and Grivois and give them apt desserts for their treachery!

It has not yet occurred to you what else the curse means – that you can never bathe or drink again. But who cares? You are a barbarian warrior! You seldom wash, and water is not your tipple of choice.

For now, you set out across the lake to get your revenge.

Turn to **73**

170

You step into the griddle-smoke, steam and clamour of the kitchen. Dozens of cooks are at work here, all preparing food for the soldiers of the fortress garrison. Almost as soon as you enter, a burly man with arms as thick as beef joints stares at you with an expression of fury. 'Get out of my kitchen!' he bellows.

If you do as he says, you can go either to the
   refectory (turn to **100**) or down the passage
   beside the kitchen (turn to **37**)
If you ignore him, turn to **33**

171

You hurry away from the fort, your strong loping
stride carrying you effortlessly ahead of your pursuers. After all, you are used to striding all day across
the wild moors of your northern homeland, while
they are bandy-legged soldiers with too much fat
around their bellies. You soon escape from them,
losing yourself in the warren of alleyways and high-
walled houses that is Tarkesh Varn.

   Turn to **79**

172

As you run, the goblins grab handfuls of snow and
hurl them after you. A futile act of petulance? Not
when the snowballs are imbued with magical force.
The moment the first snowball splatters against your
back, you feel a numbing cold spread through you.
   Roll one dice. If you get less than or equal to your
   MIND score, you shrug off the spell and escape
   from them: turn to **143**
   If you roll higher than your MIND score, the
   snowballs clump around you until you cannot
   move: turn to **163**

173

You struggle out through the surging waves and are
hauled aboard the rowboat. Few words pass between
you and the bo'sun as you return to the ship. You

watch the backs of the oarsmen as they bend to their task, breath steaming on the cold air.

Aboard the *Heldrasir* you are taken straight to see Captain Athscar, a huge white-bearded man whose ruddy face might seem jovial if it were not for his close-set eyes. His smile reminds you of ice over a pond: thin and treacherous. 'Tell me how it goes in the world?' are his first words to you.

'Eh?' You are at a loss to know what he means.

He turns and gazes at the land, dwindling now as the *Heldrasir* puts out to open sea. 'In former days a strong monarch ruled there,' he says. 'Aye, and in the lands across the ocean, too. He'd brook no opposition to his rule – crushed all contention with a fist of iron.'

'You sound as if you admired this tyrant,' you say.

The captain nods. 'Feared him, too. A man should fear his liege; it teaches respect. There are no emperors like that now, though. Weak men fill the world, splendour is humbled and glory's on its knees. What's called for now is a return to those great days of yore!'

This is worrying. The captain appears to be an arrant madman.

If you remain aboard, biding your time, turn to **27**

If you dive overboard, turn to **41**

If you threaten the captain's life, turn to **55**

174

It seems there is a sorcerer, Magister Caenwulf, who lives in a tower along the cliffs. Apparently he was a fearsome foe of Chaos in his younger days, and now that old age has made him infirm he sometimes gives aid to youthful adventurers. At least, that's the story.

In your experience sorcerers are not the sort to divvy out favours for nothing.

If you drop in on this Caenwulf, turn to **42**

If you prefer to head west without supernatural aid, turn to **147**

175

You grudgingly pay across the money and the young man shows you into the inn. (Remember to delete the appropriate sum from the total you're carrying.)

By the time he has brought out food and drink from the kitchen, your mood is less surly. Watching the gathering grey dusk over the mere, you are rather glad of the warming fire and the supper of roast pork with apples and spiced turnip-cakes. Restore one BODY point if you are wounded.

Quaffing the last drop from your tankard, you turn to the young innkeeper, whose name you have learned is Fournil. 'Do you get many travellers passing this way?' you ask him.

He pours himself a cup and joins you by the fire. 'Very few. I ascribe this to the inhospitality of the region, coupled with the devil that lives on the island in the middle of the mere.'

'A devil, you say? A foul stinking beast of the Chaos-brood? Fetch my sword, man! We will go out and face this devil at once, rather than let it come to snatch us from our beds while we sleep!'

'Wisht, and that's the ale talking!' he says with a laugh. 'There's no cause for alarm, because the waters of the mere were blessed by St Durchfaht when he passed this way many years ago. No creature of evil can cross them, you see. Our devil's stuck where he is.'

You listen as the first drops of rain start to splatter in the thatching of the roof. If you insist on venturing out on to the mere to deal with this devil, turn to **84**

If you prefer the comfort of the inn, turn to **97**

176

The punt is gone! You stare around frantically, then you catch sight of it far off in the dusk, heading rapidly towards the far shore of the lake. The treacherous pair have abandoned you!

The satyr comes crashing through the undergrowth behind you. You should have a record of his COMBAT and BODY scores. Resume your battle – but this time there is nowhere to flee.

If you win, turn to **35**

177

Note which item you have taken from this list and turn to the appropriate section to discover what it does:

The shortsword – turn to **5**

The jar of oil – turn to **72**

The magical ruby – turn to **86**

178

She holds your hand and pulls you down into the murky depths. You feel no icy chill, nor do your lungs burst for want of air, but neither of these facts surprises you. You have no time to be surprised. Instead, you are filled with wonder at the sight of the magnificent palace beneath the lake. Its marble colonnades sparkle with luminescence, revealing a sumptuous banquet laid out on silver trays. A haze of light, perhaps exuded by the star-sapphires emblazoning the upper portico, plays over fine treasures from ages past.

You dally with the maiden for a while, but you are haunted by a sense of urgency and soon you feel it is time you were on your way. She pouts, trying to tempt you to stay longer, but finally she agrees to return you to the surface.

Together you swim up to the shore of the mere. It is nearly daylight, and Grinch and Grivois are long gone. You must hope to catch up with them in the city of Tarkesh Varn, where you know they are bound.

Delete the codeword PSALMS and note down a new codeword: SNEYP.

Turn to 111

179

You can take the sergeant's own sword, if you wish. It is better than the ones in the practice hall, and will parry attacks on a roll of 1–3 on the dice (instead of the usual 1–2). He also has a pouch containing ten silver pieces. These count as a single item for encumbrance purposes.

Note down anything you're taking and then turn to 18

180

Against an experienced swordsman, your strategy is doomed to failure. Ignoring your feint, he calmly parries your sword aside and flicks his blade out as you try to dodge past him. You feel his sword-point prick the skin of your neck. You freeze. 'I yield,' you say guardedly.

Attracted by the commotion, a couple of guards rush into the practice hall. 'Be careful, sarge,' says one. 'That's the escaped prisoner.'

The sergeant smiles at you. 'Oh, not just a barbarian thief, eh? In that case, let me escort you personally to the scaffold.'

It is a short walk across the courtyard, and an even shorter drop to the end of a rope. Your adventure ends here.

181

You search high and low, but the elusive horns seem forever out of reach.

If you have a green candle and want to light it, or a pebble with a hole in it that you want to look through, or a jar of oil which you want to dab on your eyes, then turn to **117**

If you have none of those things or do not wish to use them, you have been led astray on a fruitless chase and now you must sleep out under the stars – turn to **22**

182

The next day you are approached by a group of three semi-human nomads. They wear flowing robes and sit astride the backs of odd riding beasts which resemble huge flat-snouted lizards with long legs but no forelimbs.

'Tribute!' snaps the leader of the nomads, resting his hand on the spear slung along his saddle. 'To cross our desert, a fee you must pay. Sword you have? Or silver.'

You realize that he is demanding your weapon as a toll. (If you do not have a weapon, the nomads would accept fifteen silver pieces in lieu. But if you *have* a weapon they will insist on taking that.)

If you agree to pay the toll, amend your Character
    Sheet accordingly and continue on your way by
    turning to **78**

If you have the Cloth of Marvels and wish to use it,
    turn to **101**

If you choose to defy the nomads, turn to **51**

183

Guided by a hunch, you hoist the jar up on to one of the pans. There is a scraping sound and the stone slab in front of you moves up a few centimetres. A counterweight! Hurrying back to the entrance, you bring more of the jars and load them on to the pans, their combined load gradually lifting the slab until there is room for you to duck underneath and enter the tomb of the tyrant.

Turn to **119**

184

'Ah, a quest . . .' she breathes. 'Bold warriors and stirring deeds. It reminds me of the old days, when many a man came asking me for aid. So, what help do you seek? A magic sword? A shield that reflects all sorcery? A talisman for fending off injury?'

'They'd all be handy,' you admit, 'but right now it's a simple map that I need most. A map those two scumbagulous rascals stole from me!'

You gesture towards the further shore. She looks into the thick shadows of evening. Even though Grinch and Grivois are no longer in sight, she nods and dives down into the water with hardly a sound. You wait almost a minute, and then abruptly she returns, arising from the mere in a single fluid instant.

The map is in her hand. She gives it to you. 'Those two were easy to trick,' she says with a laugh. 'Now they have a map of my devising – one that will take them to the Hall of the Sun on the far rim of the world. There they'll get their comeuppance.'

Note that you have the map back. As you put it back inside your jerkin, you say to her: 'But also, good lady, I am trapped on this island without a boat.'

With a clap of her hands, she summons huge frogs up from the mud of the lake bed. Their heads shine wet and green, slowly blinking eyes like citrines in the darkness. You look at her, lips framing a question.

'Use them as stepping stones,' she says. 'Come, I'll lead the way.' And, taking your hand, she leads you across the bobbing green heads until you finally reach the shore of the mere.

'A third boon, and then I go,' she says.

Consider what you'll ask for.

If you choose long life, turn to **190**

If you choose victory in battle, turn to **17**

185

You reach the doorway bloodied but unbowed. The guards are pouring into the kitchen behind you, but the debris of your battle delays them for a few precious seconds.

Turn to **128**

It is locked. Hearing a moan from inside, you slide open the barred aperture in the centre of the door. You peer into a cramped cell where an old man cowers miserably in chains. 'Eh?' he says weakly, looking up. 'You're not the regular gaoler . . .'

'I'm escaping,' you reply, raising a finger to your lips.

He nods, understanding. 'The guardroom is directly adjacent to this cell,' he tells you in a whisper. 'Be careful – and godspeed!'

If you have a set of keys and wish to free him, turn to **87**

If you risk entering the guardroom despite his warning, turn to **115**

Otherwise you hurry on along the passage: turn to **102**

As he lifts his own sword to deflect the blow, you suddenly weave to one side and go into a forward roll which carries you right past him and through the open doorway. Coming to your feet, you sprint off across the courtyard towards the main gate. The sergeant bellows a variety of curses at you as you go, but this seems to excite little interest from the gate guards.

Presumably, if he is anything like the sergeants you've known in your mercenary days, they are used to seeing him yell at people.

Turn to **18**

It is dusk by the time you reach Tarkesh Varn. Making your way up the steep pebble-strewn track that leads to this ancient stone fort, you see four guards resting on their spears at the gate. They give you sullen looks as you pass and one says, 'You're cutting it fine, barbarian. We'll be shutting the gates in fifteen minutes time.'

If you have the codeword PSALMS, turn to **104**

If you do not have that codeword, turn to **79**

189

You awaken close to sunset to find yourself shivering despite the lingering warmth of the day. Your tongue feels like a dead leaf, and tender red spots have broken out on your skin. You realize the dreadful truth: you have the Plague!

Your only hope of survival is a plague-curing potion. If you have such a thing you had better drink it now – cross it off your Character Sheet and turn to **182**

If you do not have the potion, turn to **137**

190

She clouts you hard between the eyes without a word of warning. Dazed, you stagger back, but the lady only laughs and says, 'That buffet has made you stronger, noble warrior.'

You realize she is right. Instead of being injured by her blow, you now have one more BODY point than you started the adventure with! Note this on your Character Sheet. Thanking the lady, you watch her disappear back into the lake.

After making yourself a bed of reeds, you pass an uncomfortable night and arise early, eager to be on your way. Delete the codeword PSALMS and then turn to **111**

At last you succeed in chipping away enough of the mortar to work one of the blocks free. By squeezing through the gap you have made in the wall, you could get into the corridor running behind your cell.

Glancing up at the narrow window-slit, you are alarmed to see that a pale silvery glow has replaced the velvet blackness of night. The guards will soon be coming for you.

If you leave the cell immediately via the exit you have made, turn to **47**

If you want to try fooling the guards, turn to **141**

If you prefer to wait and fight them, turn to **88**

192

As you take out the figurine, it comes alive in your hands and leaps to attack the serpent. The serpent responds by throwing its coils around the gold mongoose and sinking its long scimitar-shaped fangs into the valiant little creature's neck.

Fight the battle between the two:

SERPENT	COMBAT 2	BODY 9
MONGOOSE	COMBAT 6	BODY 10

If the mongoose wins, turn to **193**

If the serpent wins, it turns to you with a final spell – one that causes a roiling fog to open under your feet. Turn to **92**

193

The struggle goes on for a long time, but finally the mongoose manages to get a stranglehold on the serpent with its golden teeth, and chokes the life out of it.

You stoop to inspect the carnage. The serpent is limp and lifeless, the tyrant's soul banished to the hell he deserves. A mortal man may not have been able to defeat him, but he never considered that a simple animal might . . .

The little mongoose lies panting, close to death. The serpent's envenomed bite has proved too much for it. You watch it sadly as its last breaths slip away. Is it aware that it has just saved the world from a tyrant's rule? Or was it just doing what instinct made it do? And is that all a Hero is: someone with the instinct to fight back against evil? These are questions which are too much for a barbarian like you to answer.

Helping yourself to armfuls of loot, you begin the long journey back to civilization. It will take you months to spend this fortune in gold and gems, but spend it you will. A soft life of luxury is not for you. You know that, sooner or later, you'll feel the call of adventure again!

HEROQUEST

The Screaming Spectre

DAVE MORRIS

Listen to my words and heed them well, usurper. Your place is among the dead . . .

Strange things are afoot on the sorcerous island of Truillon. Wet floorboards and shadowy spectres suggest that the drowned Archimage has returned from the dead. Has he come to test the worthiness of his successor, or is it revenge that has called him back from his watery grave? Armed with only a strong heart and a handful of spells, the apprentice Osric must find the answers – otherwise his master is surely doomed . . .

Read carefully, for as Osric faces the dark sorceries of one who is pledged to the Great Powers of Chaos, you too must prepare yourself for a heroic adventure into the world of magic. Then take the first steps on the road to becoming a Hero by testing *your* worth as a wizard with an exciting solo scenario designed to accompany the HeroQuest game. Can *you* survive the challenge?

0 552 52776 9